4.26.78

Broadcasting and Democracy
in West Germany

Broadcasting and Democracy in West Germany

Arthur Williams

BRADFORD UNIVERSITY PRESS
in association with
CROSBY LOCKWOOD STAPLES   LONDON

Granada Publishing Limited
First published in Great Britain 1976 by
Bradford University Press in association with
Crosby Lockwood Staples
Frogmore St Albans Hertfordshire AL2 2NF and
3 Upper James Street London W1R 4BP

ISBN 0 258 96996 2

Printed in Great Britain by
Cox & Wyman Ltd
London, Fakenham and Reading

Foreword

This study of West German broadcasting, together with its
companion volume *Broadcasting and Democracy in France*, has been
generously funded by the Joseph Rowntree Social Service Trust.
In 1905, Joseph Rowntree made the remark that the best way of
influencing public opinion was through journalism. Since that
time the Trust has maintained a continuous interest in the media,
of which broadcasting has achieved an importance that could
scarcely have been foreseen in 1905. While, in Britain, the Annan
Commission is reviewing the broadcasting arrangements here, it
seemed to the authors and myself that there were some very
interesting new developments taking place in both West Germany
and France which should be investigated and made available to
English-speaking readers.

One of the litmus tests of a healthy liberal democracy is the
effectiveness of its broadcasting system. It is, however, difficult
to produce successful results because here, in contrast to the press,
the need is to maintain balance *within* one organization and not
just overall. In West Germany this is a particularly complex
matter because the country is a federation and it was decided after
the war that broadcasting should be a *Land* and not a federal
responsibility. Arthur Williams has unravelled this complex
story with great clarity and has made the subject into one of
the windows through which we can observe West German
society.

Broadcasting in the Federal Republic has been an arena of
constant struggle as the political parties have steadily extended

v

their influence. Private interests, too, have made periodic attempts to secure a foothold in the system. Two of these attempts have led to historic confrontations which throw an interesting light on the workings of democracy in Germany. The first culminated in the judgement of the Federal Constitutional Court in February 1961 which confirmed the constitutional status of broadcasting as a sphere outside the control of the state. The second was the plebiscite in Bavaria in July 1973 which prevented an overt party political takeover of public broadcasting and the introduction of private broadcasting. To force the holding of the plebiscite, 90,000 signatures were collected, mostly by young people, and a well organized campaign was conducted by leading education-ists, politicians, journalists and broadcasters. In this instance, and in the court case of 1961, it could be said that the establishment was defeated.

No attempt at comparative analysis with other countries is made in this book. Nevertheless, many of the problems facing the broadcasting networks in the advanced liberal democracies are basically the same. All of them have to face the intimate connection between their independence and a sound financial base; all of them live in some degree of tension with the political class who both covet and fear the power they hold. All of them also conduct most of their activities in public view and con-sequently need continuously to explain and justify what they are doing.

In West Germany, as in Britain, the party system operates in an essentially 'bipolar' fashion in which an often artificial con-frontation between two points of view becomes accepted practice. In these circumstances it is of vital importance that a democracy has the antidote of an effective public voice free from party political pressures. In France the main problem has been that the government in office has had too great a control over broadcasting and has been able greatly to restrict the access of the voters to the views of the opposition. In Germany the danger is not that the governing party is getting too great a degree of control, but that politicians as a class are moving into this position. Public dis-cussion on the great issues of the day can never be left to politic-ians, however ready they may always be to start up a fresh argument. On many occasions, even politicians of different parties have identical interests, such as the desire that there should *not* be a discussion about something. Machinery to protect voters from these situations will always be needed, for, as John Stuart Mill said in his famous essay *On Liberty*: 'While every one well knows himself to be fallible, few think it necessary to take any precautions against their own fallibility . . .'

Stephen Holt
Professor of European Studies
University of Bradford

Acknowledgements

Resources and materials in a new university, particularly in a field which is new also outside that university, are of necessity limited; a work of the present kind could not have been contemplated without considerable help from many quarters. The basic research, of which this book is one product, was financed by the Joseph Rowntree Social Trust Ltd. I wish to express, also on behalf of the University of Bradford, sincere thanks to the trustees for the generous and understanding assistance they have given. Without their support neither this book nor the companion volume on French broadcasting would have been completed.

Professor S. C. Holt, Professor of European Studies in the University of Bradford, was instrumental in making the research for, and the publication of this book possible. I thank him for this and for the considerable personal effort he has often made on my behalf at times not always convenient to him.

Miss Charmian Richards was, for the first year of the work on this project, my research assistant. Miss Richards was able to travel in my stead to Germany and it is to her efforts that the collection of all but a very small portion of the basic material must be attributed.* I am indebted to her for the excellent corpus of material she provided and for the long and stimulating dis-

* Miss Richards has also been able to pursue her own research interests in West German broadcasting. It is hoped that her thesis on the relationship of the democratic principle to the production situation within the broadcasting stations will be completed in the near future.

cussions on the more difficult and fascinating aspects of this work.

All the West German broadcasting authorities have been most helpful in answering queries and supplying documents; I am grateful for the assistance received from them. I should like to record my appreciation for the efforts made on our behalf by the staff of the information offices, in particular, of the *Arbeitsgemeinschaft der öffentlich-rechtlichen Rundfunkanstalten der Bundesrepublik Deutschland, Bayerischer Rundfunk, Hessischer Rundfunk, Saarländischer Rundfunk, Südwestfunk* and *Zweites Deutsches Fernsehen*. The staff of the *Deutsches Rundfunkarchiv* (Frankfurt-am-Main) and of the *ZDF Historisches Hausarchiv* (Mainz) have obliged us with many services and shown us constant good will; I thank them for their genuine interest in the work carried out in Bradford.

Because of the nature of the work, great demands have been made on library facilities and resources; my admiration for the patience and hard work of the staff of the Social Sciences Library in the University of Bradford and of their colleagues elsewhere who have assisted through the Inter-Library Loan service is wholehearted. I want particularly to thank Mr J. J. Horton, the Social Sciences Librarian, who in the past months has often been my best friend.

The production of a book of this kind is no easy matter in a department where great emphasis is placed on teaching and where the students are always, to their credit, very much in evidence. The support of Professor F. M. Willis, Director of the Modern Languages Centre, of my head of department, Professor R. B. Tilford, and of my immediate colleagues, and the allowances they and my students have made for me, have been greatly appreciated.

Much has gone into the making of this book that cannot be ascribed directly to individuals; it is in this sense a tribute to the people to whom I owe so much, my teachers and friends. Some people have, however, helped materially by reading the typescript and offering useful comment, and I am grateful for their sacrifice of time and for their interest: Mr D. K. Allen, Mr P. Clark, Miss J. E. Harmer, Miss P. A. Haslett, Mr A. R. Lawson, Miss S. E. A. Parsons, Mr R. J. Robinson, Mrs I. B. Rock, Mr B. Shaw and, last but not least, Miss R. M. Welch.

I am grateful to the officers of the University of Bradford Press and to Crosby Lockwood Staples for their interest in the present work and for their invaluable advice and assistance in the preparation of its final form.

Finally, I owe a profound debt of gratitude to my wife who, in addition to her many sacrifices, has found the time to read and comment on my work. I have been particularly grateful for her forbearance and long-suffering in her countless sorties to rescue me from the attentions of the phantom typist – to whom I dedicate this book.

A. Williams
October 1975

Preface

Broadcasting and Democracy in West Germany has been written to meet a very real need in the material available to students and teachers of German in the newer institutions of higher education. Courses in languages of the type taught in the Modern Languages Centre of the University of Bradford attempt to combine the development of high-grade, practical language skills with the acquisition of relevant and useful knowledge about the societies and cultures of the respective countries. They hope to engender in their students a continuing interest for and a deepening insight into the interrelationships of language, institutions and culture – which are, ultimately, indivisible. The translator or interpreter depends for his success on a broad knowledge and ready understanding of the mind of the people of whose language he is master; he is an expert in the contemporary language and the contemporary society of the country he studies.

In the language field the challenge has been to find new methods for and new attitudes to the teaching and use of language skills; in the field of society the problem is to search out relevant material and to present it in an accessible form, in a form that is meaningful to the student who is primarily a linguist, who is not a political scientist, an economist, a sociologist, but who needs to appreciate aspects of the work of all of these in relation to a particular situation: life in the country of his chosen language. There is very little material that is directly useful to the teacher and student of contemporary society which has been collected together in a concise and readable form. This book attempts to provide an answer to this problem in respect of one aspect of German studies.

Although in this sense its scope is limited, and its structure has been determined largely by this objective, the book has nevertheless other aims which should be noted. It offers an opportunity for economies in teaching time by providing in one volume essential information and some hints at where the student can take up individual research. Where in the standard 'contemporary society' course a few hours only can be devoted to the study of the mass media, now with this volume as support material this valuable time can be used to probe and explore the wider implications of the broadcasting media in contemporary West German society; the undergraduate student has here most, if not all, of what he needs to know about West German broadcasting. Above and beyond this he has in the present volume, because it attempts to relate broadcasting to the society it serves, a presentation of West German society through an examination of one institution; he will not be able to read this little book without applying his mind to, for example, the implications of federal structures, or the problems of the education system.

Because the volume represents an attempt to go beyond what is simply West German broadcasting, it is hoped that a more general readership will find it both instructive and stimulating.

The book is complete in itself and yet, because the study of any society can never pretend to be in any way definitive, it does not aim ever to be the sole point of reference. For this reason, the sources quoted have been chosen because they can be fairly readily available to the reader, who is recommended to look further into these and beyond. Sources that cannot be followed up conveniently, interviews and the like, have not been incorporated into the present work. Similarly, where several sources are available to illustrate a given point, the most accessible have been quoted. For example, the various broadcasting laws have been kindly supplied by, and could be obtained from the broadcasting authorities themselves, but for ease of reference the excellent collection of documents edited by Wolfgang Lehr and Klaus Berg has been quoted as the standard text. It is hoped that the reader will turn to this volume for further documentary evidence; for further general reading, in particular, the ARD yearbooks and

Heiko Flottau's very readable little account can be thoroughly recommended.

Many of the readers of *Broadcasting and Democracy in West Germany* will have some knowledge of German; however, it seemed unreasonable to expect any but a select few to have a command of the German language great enough to cope with the difficulties of many of the passages quoted. All quotations have, therefore, been translated into English by the author – the sole exception being the few clauses quoted from the Basic Law. In preparing the translations the author was guided by the need to make otherwise inaccessible material available to the general reader; the translations are functional, they do not aspire to be literary masterpieces; some are literal in the extreme, others are far from literal. Some of the translations will puzzle the Germanist with a love of translation – the author would take great delight in any debate that might arise from them; in the end, they must be accepted for what they are – an aid to the reader. Where it was felt that the reader with a knowledge of German would be helped by the additional information, the original German for individual words has occasionally been supplied in parenthesis.

No matter how firm the resolve to translate everything into English, there is a limit to this exercise. Although here this limit has been somewhat stretched, it is the author's view that one word in particular loses too much in translation: *Land* and its plural, *Länder*. To talk of the 'states' (except, perhaps, in respect of Bavaria) in the context of modern Germany is to rob these administrative units of much of their significance and is often confusing. Similarly *Bund* has been kept in many instances – although it must be confessed that this was something of a device for convenience to avoid the long-winded explanation about the 'administrative organization(s) of the federal government' which would have had to serve as a translation. The temptation to leave two other, often repeated titles in the original was great: *Intendant(en)* and *Ministerpräsident(en)*. For the latter, for ease of reading, it was decided that the translation 'prime minister(s) (of the *Länder*)' should be risked. For *Intendant*, since the word seems to exist in English for use specifically in the sort of context found here, and because director-general can be misleading and difficult in use, 'intendant' has been kept. Where it seemed possible and helpful, the names of the *Länder* have been translated;

'Hessen' has been kept, rather than the so often mispronounced 'Hesse', to ensure that the two syllables of the German are respected.

The book is offered as a practical contribution to the modern study of Germany and German; it is hoped that in this sense it will serve.

Contents

Abbreviations

ARD   *Arbeitsgemeinschaft der öffentlich-rechtlichen Rundfunkan-stalten der Bundesrepublik Deutschland* (the association of the West German public broadcasting corporations – see page 15)

BR   *Bayerischer Rundfunk* (Bavarian Broadcasting Corporation, Munich)

DFS   *Deutsches Fernsehen* (the first television channel)

DLF   *Deutschlandfunk* (long-wave radio station broadcasting for European listeners)

DW   *Deutsche Welle* (short-wave radio station broadcasting a world service)

EBU   *European Broadcasting Union*

HR   *Hessischer Rundfunk* (Hessen Broadcasting Corporation, Frankfurt-am-Main)

NDR   *Norddeutscher Rundfunk* (North German Broadcasting Corporation, Hamburg)

NWDR   *Nordwestdeutscher Rundfunk* (North-West German Broadcasting Corporation – no longer exists)

RB   *Radio Bremen*

RIAS   *Rundfunk im amerikanischen Sektor von Berlin* (Radio in the American Sector of Berlin)

SDR   *Süddeutscher Rundfunk* (South German Broadcasting Corporation, Stuttgart)

SFB   *Sender Freies Berlin* (freely translated: Radio Free Berlin, West Berlin)

SR   *Saarländischer Rundfunk* (Broadcasting Corporation of the Saar, Saarbrücken)

SWF *Südwestfunk* (South-West Broadcasting Corporation, Baden-Baden)

WDR *Westdeutscher Rundfunk* (West German Broadcasting Corporation, Cologne)

ZDF *Zweites Deutsches Fernsehen* (Second German television station, Mainz)

Introduction

It is almost a truism to observe that a nation gets the leaders it deserves, and equally that a society gets the institutions it deserves. Institutions, like leaders, are products of circumstances in society and are not easily explained or understood in isolation from these circumstances; institutions are also, like leaders, forces for conservation – holding a society together – and vehicles for development – providing a basis for change and progress. As the institutions supporting and defining a society change, so they indicate changes that have already occurred in that society and offer at the same time a hint of changes to come.

No institutions reflect the character of a society more immediately than, perhaps, the media of communication and articulation; essentially they bind society together. Communication and articulation cannot take place outside the complex set of relations that constitute the society they are part of and form. Communication and articulation, the media of communication and articulation, are of the tissue of society. The definition of one is at once the definition of the other. The discussion of one of the media of mass communication is perforce a mediate discussion of the society that maintains it; the analysis and evaluation of an indigenous medium or system of mass communication is, similarly, no more and no less than a society looking at itself, defining its own characteristics and aims and, in the process, creating the foundation for its own future.

An examination of the West German broadcasting system is, therefore, indirectly an exploration of the state of society in the

Federal Republic. Within the framework of a discussion of West German broadcasting there will, of course, be no opportunity, nor would it be appropriate, to explore the ramifications of the social, economic and political questions that must inevitably be touched upon; but in limiting the discussion to one aspect of society, in attempting to take broadcasting to some extent out of its societal context, the issue of the quality of that society is in no way ducked. It is hoped that the isolation of one part of the system, certainly of so essential a part, will provide a clearer view of the fundamental character of the society, of its development over the period under review, than many a necessarily inadequate attempt to portray 'West German Society' as a whole. This discussion of broadcasting in the Federal Republic is inevitably a comment on the development of West Germany since the war; the discussion of the problems of broadcasting and the way they have (or have not) been resolved is a revealing and thoroughly valid statement on the functioning and maturity, of the state of the West German economic, social and political mind.

The work that follows is then a statement about, a comment on West German society – not a definitive one and one without the pretension to completeness; it pretends to outline one more facet, to pose another set of problems, to provide (perhaps its one ambition) a stimulus to look again and to look further.

It could be argued that an examination of the development of the broadcasting system constitutes a statement about how far the Germans in the west have absorbed the lessons of the past; how far the defeat, partition, reconstruction, the years of suspicious scrutiny, the years of probation have been effective in forming a new German society with its own reserves of strength. The problems and conflicts within and surrounding the broadcasting system have been and are a good test of whether the Germans in the Federal Republic have developed in their public lives the moral strength to survive the normal, day-to-day crises of the western, democratic way of life.

It would, perhaps, be not inappropriate to risk a sweeping statement to lend some force to the parallel between developments in the broadcasting system and in society at large in the Federal Republic. Two turning-points in West German political life have been marked by events in the world of broadcasting.

In the early 1960s the first real change in West German politics, the ending of the Adenauer era and the opening of the centre of the arena to the Social Democrats, came after three events which coupled defeat for the government with a serious loss of public face: the television ruling of the Constitutional Court (28 February 1961), the building of the Berlin Wall (13 August 1961) and the *Spiegel* affair (October–November 1962). If any events have redressed the balance and begun to establish respect for Germany and its politicians, they have been recent, separated from the first three by a decade: the signing of the treaties with the eastern European states and particularly with the German Democratic Republic (26 May 1972), the failure of the vote of no confidence in Chancellor Brandt and the resultant appeal to the people (September–November 1972), Brandt's resignation (6 May 1974) and the manner in which *Bundestag* procedures were adapted to allow a proper discussion of the highly controversial question of the legalization of abortion (26 April 1974). If these are signs that West Germany has taken a step forward in its development towards full majority in the world of politics (both national and international), if they are signs of growing maturity, then again they have a proper parallel in the world of broadcasting – not a government defeat in the Constitutional Court, instead a genuinely popular movement which forced the hand of the ruling party in Bavaria, winning the restitution of a pluralistic broadcasting law (culminating on 1 August 1973).

There is more than mild appropriateness in the terms 'life-nerve of democracy' and 'obstetrician of majority'[1] when applied to the broadcasting media in the Federal Republic. In their attitude to these media, whether it be expressed in laws, rulings of the Constitutional Court, political manœuvrings, popular actions or economic measures, the West Germans have over the years revealed their attitude to a fundamental vehicle of democracy – to what is now seen by at least one of their political parties as the vehicle for, and therefore guardian of, the most fundamental of human rights. In the preamble to their paper on the media, the Free Democrats said:

> The basic right of the freedom of opinion, of information and of the press is not a basic right alongside others. (It is) of central importance for the preservation and exercise of all other basic rights.[2]

The account of the West German broadcasting system that follows is then something of an investigation of the attitude of the people of West Germany to the most fundamental of the basic rights, an examination of the democratic nerve of the Federal Republic, an observation of the quality of the society born of the Federal Republic.

Part One

The Allies and West German Broadcasting

After the German capitulation in May 1945 and the assumption of full occupation rights over Germany by the victorious allies, all power to make decisions and take effective measures to mould the future shape of Germany was wrested from the Germans, who were allowed to participate in the planning for the rebuilding of life in Germany initially only under conditions of strictest control and generally only to formulae predetermined by the powers of occupation. There has been much debate about the proper significance of the various steps that culminated with the division of Germany into two states; what is clear in retrospect is that the unanimity between the allies of east and west, much vaunted in the joint communiqués of the wartime and immediately postwar period, was hardly deep enough to hold out hope of implementation in practice. The western allies themselves often pulled in different directions and entertained several clearly contradictory views about the treatment to be meted out to the vanquished enemy.

The Four Powers did, however, envisage a change of structures to eliminate every possibility of a return by Germany to past forms of government and control; the change was attempted in both parts of Germany, albeit with different emphases. In the east a fundamental part of the 'socialist' solution was the complete reform of patterns of ownership over economic resources, coupled with the imposition of an authoritarian government system controlled largely from without. The western allies, rejecting the Morgenthau attitude and endorsing the Marshall approach, re-invested many of the old bases of the economy with new, even added power and made the focal point of their effort to bury the German past the reform of political structures and attitudes.

One point on which the Three Powers had agreed at Potsdam was the need for a decentralization of power in Germany, both administrative and economic. The division of Germany into zones of occupation served in itself to promote a decentralization and differentiation of the system, the few common administrative areas having a largely service function; and they were short-lived. Within their zones the western allies, the Americans in particular, tended to organize administration with the *Land* as the largest unit – and with some striking differences in approach. These differences were a result of two main factors: the ideals and predilections of the occupying power, and the characteristics of the region in question. In respect of the mass media, for example, the British and the Americans applied very different rules in the licensing of news organs: the British promoted newspapers of distinctive party colouring and soon catered fully for the large, predominantly concentrated, urban population of their zone; the Americans nullified the effects of party politics by licensing papers to editorial boards composed of people representing several, not always compatible shades of opinion and failed to cater fully for their population which was scattered generally in small pockets of rural communities – it was in the American zone that the greatest proliferation of news organs occurred when licensing restrictions were lifted in 1949.

Thus the pattern was set for a largely decentralized system in the western zones, a pattern that could not easily be influenced by the conjoining of the three zones and the founding of the West German state, the form of which was itself not left to the Germans to devise – although they were empowered through representatives of the *Länder* to frame its constitution within guidelines set by the allies:

> The delegates to this (constitution-framing) Assembly will be elected in each *Land* in accordance with procedures and regulations still to be decided by the legislative bodies in the individual states. This constitution is to make it possible for the Germans themselves to contribute to the ending of the present division of Germany not by the re-establishment of a centrally governed *Reich*, but by a federal

government which adequately protects the rights of the individual states, provides at the same time for an adequate central body and guarantees the rights and freedoms of the individual.[1]

It is open to speculation whether the framers of the constitution were guided more by the exhortations of the allies or the spectre of the weaknesses of the Weimar constitution. The Basic Law that was the outcome of their deliberations is federal, does protect the rights of the individual states and of the individual citizen and goes a long way towards correcting the insufficiencies of the Weimar balance of power at the centre.

The framers of the Basic Law, keenly aware of their role as representatives of the *Länder*, took pains to define the division of competence between the federal government and the individual *Land* governments. In addition to two general statements in the second section of the Basic Law, 'The exercise of governmental powers and the discharge of governmental functions is incumbent upon the *Länder* in so far as this Basic Law does not otherwise prescribe or permit' and 'Federal law overrides *Land* law',[2] articles 70–75 elucidate in detail the distinction to be made between areas in which the *Bund* (the federal government) has the exclusive right of legislation, areas in which legislation is said to be concurrent (where the *Länder* may legislate as long as the *Bund* does not) and the third area of legislation where the *Bund* may enact a framework law, leaving the details of its implementation to the *Länder*. These articles list the areas of government that fall into each category – all other fields are the province of *Land* legislation.

Nowhere in these articles is reference made to broadcasting. Legislation in the field of broadcasting is the prerogative of the *Länder*, provided that any such legislation does not infringe the basic constitutional rights of the individual or endanger the constitutional status of the Federal Republic. In the whole of the Basic Law one reference only is made to broadcasting, in article five in the first section where the basic rights of the individual are set out. The reference here is of fundamental importance:

> Everyone has the right freely to express and to disseminate his opinion by speech, writing and pictures and freely to inform himself from generally accessible sources. Freedom of the press and freedom of reporting by radio and motion pictures are guaranteed. There shall be no censorship.[3]

[9]

In the original the term used for 'radio' is *Rundfunk*, which is general and can embrace television as well as radio and is now more usefully translated in most contexts by 'broadcasting'.

It was 1961 before the case for sole responsibility in broadcasting was fully tested and definitively resolved in favour of the *Länder*. Then, however, the point at issue was not the establishment of a basic broadcasting system, but the addition to the already highly developed system of a second television programme. The broadcasting system as it exists in West Germany today was founded in most of its essential features in the period of the occupation. The western allies provided the German people with all the tools necessary for the practice of pluralistic democracy, a book of rules and some guidance in their implementation.

There are nine regional broadcasting stations in the Federal Republic today, a 'second' television station (ZDF) and two 'cultural' radio stations (DW, DLF). Of the nine regional stations four are the stations founded by the Americans and a fifth by the French. The British, who like the French took as a model their home centralized system, founded the sixth station of the occupation period, the massive NWDR in Hamburg, to cater for the whole of their zone and the British sector in Berlin. Subsequently NWDR split into two, NDR in Hamburg and WDR in Cologne, and the Berlin studio became part of SFB. The ninth station broadcasting today is the Saarland station (SR), a later foundation. The system bequeathed to the Germans by the allies was hardly balanced in terms of the requirements of the Federal Republic as a whole; it is unlikely that a centrally planned system would, for example, have included a small station like *Radio Bremen* on the doorstep of the giant NDR in Hamburg.

The allies endowed the German broadcasting system with rather more than technical installations located in not always the best sites; they also gave their stations constitutions which had all the characteristics still in evidence in the constitutions of today's stations, governed now by *Land* legislation. All broadcasting stations are corporations of public law with constitutional control everywhere in the hands of representatives of the public and nowhere the prerogative of a government or of a single interest. Nearly all have a three-tier system of control comprising the broadcasting council, the administrative council and the intendant.

All are financed mainly from licence fees collected by the Federal Post Office (this latter arrangement will change in 1976). Thus the allies gave the German people a federal broadcasting system founded on the principle of serving the public at large and protected by law from the influence of the state; an important contribution to the practical re-education of the German political mind.

An additional bonus for the public claim to control all broadcasting in the Federal Republic was contained in the circumspect formulation of the British station's constitution.[4] This contains in paragraph one of its first section an interesting parenthesis: 'The broadcasts are to provide in word and music (later, as soon as technically possible, also in pictures) entertainment, education, enlightenment and information'; and this in conjunction with a clear statement of the station's legally protected monopoly of broadcasting in the whole area of the British zone:

> The purpose of the North-West German Broadcasting Corporation is the sole control of all presently existing and future broadcasting installations (including wired radio) in the *Länder* North Rhine-Westphalia, Lower Saxony, Schleswig-Holstein and the Hanseatic City of Hamburg.

NWDR had a monopoly of broadcasting extending to future innovations including television. Nor was it a coincidence that these clauses were written into the NWDR constitution; it was the largest and richest station and was also fortunate enough to have access to the only radio installations preserved intact from the war and to most of the television equipment salvaged. It was the only station in a position to take up experimental work in television at that time, its sole potential rival being the central organ of administration, the *Deutsche Post*; and NWDR had a binding agreement with the Post Office permitting it to carry out its experiments. The *Land* authorities, once they had assumed legal responsibility for broadcasting, were in a very strong position to repulse the advances of the federal government into this field at a later date.

It was in the field of television, where the extreme differences between the stations in size and resources made equal progress by all of them and competition between them impossible, that co-operation and exchange proved an obvious material benefit. The stations practised a high degree of co-operation in both radio and television from the earliest days – a process that might have developed less rapidly and less successfully had the stations been established, for example, by independent groups competing for the same public. As the stations emerged under the influence of the allies each could be confident of its incontestable legal autonomy and assured of its public. They had a common constitutional objective – the service of the public; this and the common enemy which was to emerge, the central government, helped them to forge bonds of mutual aid which have become the strength of the system.

CHAPTER TWO

Federalism in West German Broadcasting

THE BROADCASTING STATIONS AND THE
FOUNDING OF ARD

Radio Hamburg was the first radio station to start broadcasting in Germany at the end of the war on 4 May 1945. From this time until 22 July 1949, when *Radio Stuttgart* was finally transferred from American to German control and became SDR, public broadcasting in West Germany was supervised to a greater or lesser extent by the allies. A remarkable feature is that responsibility in broadcasting was returned to the Germans after only a very short period; German personnel were employed in all six stations from the beginning and all the stations except the British had German intendants by the end of 1947. Although Hugh Carleton Greene remained at the helm of NWDR until mid November 1948, the British station was effectively German from late 1945 and was the first station to be returned to the Germans by law (1 January 1948, in pursuance of Military Regulation No. 118 of 30 August 1947). The retention of a British adviser at the head of the station was an expression of the determination of both sides to set firm foundations for the new German broadcasting system. (The arrangement has its parallel in the administration of the 'British' newspaper *Die Welt*.)

The pattern of transfer from allied to German control was roughly the same for all six stations: a short period as a military transmitter, rapid employment of German personnel and granting of responsibilities to them, then the transfer of full control to the

German authorities. The only station where the process was held up somewhat by the occupation authorities was *Radio Stuttgart*, where the intervention of the American authorities prevented the passing of the first broadcasting law by the *Landtag* in August 1948. The Federal Republic, however, did not become a fully sovereign state until 1955 when the occupation was finally terminated; the Allied High Commission, in fact, retained some nominal control over the mass media until that time. The Allied Press and Broadcasting Law of 21 September 1949 gave the High Commission access to the media on request and prohibited the publication of material detrimental to the allies' interests. The High Commission reserved the right to determine whether new broadcasting stations should be set up or not. First and foremost, however, the law established the rights of the High Commission to protect the freedom of information in West Germany; article one reads:

> As is provided in the Basic Law, the German press, radio and other information services are free. The Allied High Commission reserves the right to rescind or nullify any measure, be it a political, adminis-trative or financial measure of government, which threatens this freedom.[1]

The main concern of the allies is quite unambiguously stated; it needs no further emphasis.

Although all the broadcasting stations had the same legal status as bodies corporate of public law, they were constituted after the transfer of control in two different ways reflecting the federal system of *Land* autonomy. The stations which served one *Land* only were constituted by the enactment of a *Land* law, while the stations which served more than one *Land*, the British NWDR and the French SWF, were constituted by inter-*Land* agreements. In 1954 North Rhine-Westphalia decided to secede from the NWDR agreement and constitute its own WDR in Cologne; the remaining three *Länder* concluded a new agreement to found NDR. In mid 1954 the NWDR studio in Berlin was handed over to SFB, which the Berlin Senate had been allowed to constitute in late 1953. The French supra-*Land* station, SWF, still serves the same areas as at the time of its initial foundation (Rhineland-Palatinate and the southern part of Baden-Württemberg as they are now) and has its legal basis in the inter-*Land* agreement of 1951 between Rhineland–

Palatinate, Baden and Württemberg–Hohenzollern. The northern part of what is now Baden-Württemberg is served by SDR. At present six stations serve an area defined by the administrative boundaries of the relevant *Land* (BR, HR, RB, SR, SFB and WDR), one serves three distinct *Länder* (NDR), one serves one *Land* and part of another (SWF) and one serves part only of one *Land* (SDR). The situation implies that there is in some areas considerable co-operation between individual *Länder* in the interests of an effective public broadcasting service; the opening of the second television service (ZDF) in 1963, which was made possible by an inter-*Land* agreement between all the West German *Länder*, provides a later but conclusive example of the effectiveness of the same spirit. The most fundamental endorsement of the federalistic ideal came from the broadcasting stations themselves when they joined forces in 1950 to form their *Arbeitsgemeinschaft der öffentlich-rechtlichen–Rundfunkanstalten der Bundesrepublik Deutschland*, known universally since early 1955 as ARD (the abbreviation was used for EBU purposes in late 1954 and then introduced internally in the Federal Republic).

The ARD title was carefully chosen to denote the relationship that the broadcasting authorities were creating among themselves; the German is so deliberately precise that it defies effective translation. It can be translated, but in no way elegantly. In his book *The Mass Media*, Stuart Hood gives as the English version: 'Consortium of the Chartered Broadcasting Companies of the Federal Republic of Germany.'[2] Two words leave some doubt as to their final accuracy – quintessential here: 'consortium' and 'company'. Both are associated too closely with the language of trade and commerce to be really applicable here. *Arbeitsgemeinschaft* can mean simply a 'study group', but more often means some form of joint association formed to achieve a common objective, with the only link between the members the achievement of this objective. 'Syndicate' or 'consortium' will translate the word in some contexts, but the simpler idea of an 'association' is a better starting point. Here the emphasis is clearly on the designation of the broadcasting authorities as *öffentlich-rechtlich*, on their status as independent, sovereign bodies; they are 'bodies corporate of public law', 'public corporations'. These public corporations have allied themselves together to pursue more effectively the aim they share of providing the public with a free broadcasting service, free of any predominant political or commercial interests. The result: a federation of the public broadcasting corporations of the Federal Republic of Germany.

The care that went into the choice of a name for the institutionalized co-operation of the West German broadcasting authorities is a good indication of the achievement it represents, coming as it did at a time when the allies, the public and above all the broadcasters themselves mistrusted any form of centralization in the media. The form the alliance took is a symbol of this mistrust.

The notice to the press announcing the founding of the ARD was issued on 5 August 1950 after the individual intendants had had time to discuss within their supervisory bodies and with their legal experts the terms of the constitution put to them at their meeting held on 9–10 June 1950. This latter date is generally associated with the founding of the ARD. By mid 1950, however, the heads of the stations had been meeting to discuss points of common interest at irregular intervals for a full four years. The four stations in the American zone, together with RIAS, had most in common and had least problems of inter-zonal travel and so met regularly, in particular to discuss their broadcasts for schools. Education was a topic (standard contracts, terms for the exchange of material were others) which was of importance to all the stations in the western zones and, initially, also to their East German colleagues; representatives of all of them did, in fact, meet in Berlin in November 1946 and again in September 1947 in Munich.

The jealousy with which the stations guarded their independence and resisted any move that would give even an appearance of uniformity and incipient centralism is well illustrated by the fact that conferences were organized in such a way that representatives of the different controlling bodies of the stations never attended the same conference. The intendants met as one group, the chairmen of the administrative councils as another. It was feared that a joint meeting of both groups would, in any policy decision, speak almost with the voice of a central broadcasting authority. The emergence of the Federal Republic and the concomitant threat of federal legislation for broadcasting eventually forced the two groups to formalize the inter-station co-operation. The broadcasting authorities needed to speak with one voice to protect their interests, to preserve their independence.

The founding of the ARD marks the beginning of the new age in German broadcasting and, interestingly enough, it involved a symbolic defeat for the old order at the hands of the new. The old order could be said to be represented in particular by the figure of Hans Bredow, then chairman of the HR administrative council, and the new by the leading figures in NWDR, Hugh Carleton Greene, Adolf Grimme (intendant) and Hans Brack (legal adviser). The differences between them were in approach and emphasis.

Bredow,[3] who had been instrumental in building the omnipotent *Reichsrundfunkgesellschaft* (German Broadcasting Company) before his dismissal by the Nazis, played the role in the postwar situation of the experienced and forceful theorist not quite in touch with changed circumstances. His ideas were sound in principle, but inappropriate in practice. His ideal was a broadcasting service as a bastion of education, culture and entertainment for the whole of Germany. He suggested to the allies a division of power within the stations between two legal entities – a principle adopted everywhere in the division between the public supervision and the station. In this context the emphasis that was not accepted was his relegation of the intendant to a position of purely executive subordination to the powerful chairmen of the councils, particularly of the administrative council.

By 1949 Bredow had seen the need for unity between the six broadcasting authorities; he set out to try to achieve this, in the process attempting to shift the emphasis at the top of the system away from the intendants and towards the chairmen of the administrative councils. He organized meetings of these latter and even succeeded in bringing about joint meetings of the intendants with the chairmen of both the administrative and broadcasting councils (particularly 6–7 December 1949). The role of the intendant was by that time firmly established so that Bredow's moves caused not a little resentment. His idea of unity was also unwelcome in the form he seemed to be suggesting: an *Arbeitsgemeinschaft* set up by the chairmen of the administrative councils with the name *Deutscher Rundfunk* – truly a 'German broadcasting consortium'. Bredow insisted that he had the interests of public broadcasting at heart (none would deny this); he called for unity to offset the threat of unity of a different kind that was becoming apparent in central government circles.

Joint meetings of the chairmen and the intendants have continued to be held without any loss of status on the part of the intendants, and unity was achieved – but not in the form suggested by Bredow. He was instrumental in making his colleagues think about problems of importance, but not in leading them to the solution required by the times; his actions had the effect of increasing unity among the intendants and pushing them towards the proposals submitted by the NWDR representatives. Bredow did nothing ultimately that was not in the interests of the system; he stimulated debate and increased the broadcasters' clarity of vision at a critical moment.

Bredow's action probably expedited the founding of the ARD; he created the right climate of discussion for Dr Grimme to reintroduce the proposals drawn up some time earlier by Dr Brack at Hugh Carleton Greene's instigation. The latter had, like Dr Bredow, seen the need for some form of institutionalized unity and although in 1950 he was himself no longer in a position to implement his ideas, he had provided the blueprint which, reviewed and modified by more general discussion, the intendants accepted (with the approval of their home authorities) as the basis for the constitution of the ARD.

THE ARD CONSTITUTION

The terms under which the broadcasting stations agreed to found their joint association in 1950 are a charter of pluralism in practice. Between 1950 and 1962, as the ARD constitution underwent gradual modification, the underlying testimony to independence and co-operation embodied in it emerged with increasing vigour. The constitution shows that the will of the West German broadcasting authorities to co-operation and mutual aid is great, the determination to resist any infringement of their individual sovereignty even greater.

Unlike a binding contract formulated at great length in generally incomprehensible legal minutiae, the ARD constitution is short and pellucid;[4] it is intended to be open and flexible, respecting the status and good sense of the members. The only absolute obligation the ARD as a body seems to impose on the members requires the individual authorities to provide full information in areas relevant to the work of the ARD. This (§7) and the preceding paragraph testify to the spirit of the association: 'The financial means required for the implementation of the resolutions of the *Arbeitsgemeinschaft*[5] are provided by the members according to their ability to pay' (§6).

Any broadcasting body in the Federal Republic can associate itself with the ARD, provided that it is a properly constituted public corporation; conversely any member can withdraw after a year's notification – a necessary safeguard for joint ventures since planning in broadcasting on this scale can hardly be undertaken for shorter periods. Membership of ARD in no way affects arrangements between the individual authorities, nor does it impose financial obligations on the members for projects they do not specifically endorse.

The ARD has set itself four main tasks which are outlined in §2(1):

(a) to safeguard the common interests of the broadcasting authorities in the exercise of sovereign rights in the area of broadcasting;
(b) to safeguard other common interests of the broadcasting authorities;
(c) to deal with common questions of programming and common questions of a legal and technical nature and of business management;
(d) to provide expert reports on questions which arise from the interpretation and application of regulations relevant to the individual stations which are of general significance ...

Flexibility is again the key: the paragraph ends with the simple statement that the members decide what questions shall be dealt with and whether any further areas of activity shall be added.

For the rest, the constitution sets out the rules for convening the two types of assembly, full (attended by intendants and chairmen) and working (intendants only), and for the procedures to be observed in the adoption of various kinds of resolution; it provides for the rotation of the chairmanship and, with this, of the administration from station to station, and empowers the assembly to delegate functions of representation as required.

The constitution is no more than a bare framework for the work of the ARD; the full value of the association becomes more apparent in the armoury of supplementary agreements that the members have entered into, covering *inter alia* finance, common radio and television programmes and co-operation with ZDF, and also in the ARD sponsorship of a few technical institutions that support it in its work. Its work is further facilitated by a battery of standing and *ad hoc* commissions and committees, each with the right to set up sub-committees and working parties. Finally, the ARD embraces the *Gesamtrat*, a name which readily conjures echoes of Bredow; it comprises representatives of all the controlling bodies of all the broadcasting authorities – it is the combined, or collective, broadcasting council of all the stations. Its function is far removed from anything that Bredow might have wished: it undertakes expert investigations, if it considers the work worthwhile, in any area requested by one or more of the ARD members. These investigations can be financed by the ARD but the commissioning body is usually expected to pay.

THE FEDERAL GOVERNMENT AND PLURALISM IN BROADCASTING

The broadcasting authorities formed their own central association as an embodiment of their ideal of pluralism under the pressure of a threat of a different kind of centralism – and hardly a moment too soon, for the next decade was to be virtually a running battle between, on the one side, the broadcasting authorities and the *Länder* and, on the other, the central government. In this period, up to 1961, the West German broadcasting system took on its definitive shape in terms both of networks and of legislation.

After exploratory discussions in 1950, the first serious sparring seems to have come on 9 May 1951 when various voices were heard in the *Bundestag* both for and against the idea of federal legislation on broadcasting.[6] All sides conceded the need to respect the status of the *Länder* and the opposition to a *Bund* move in this field came from the SPD and the Bavarian Party (*Bayernpartei*).

The main arguments put forward by government speakers can be summarized briefly: standardization was necessary to promote neutrality and fairness in the running of the stations; central control of finance would simplify the business of licensing and help to even out differences in financial status between the stations; research also could be centralized to advantage, particularly in the important field of television. There was a strong case to be argued for the existence of a single German voice in the international world (say, at conferences when negotiations of equal importance for all the regions were to be conducted) and also to represent the Federal Republic on the air – especially to counter propaganda from the GDR. Some deputies suggested that a central voice was also needed internally to protect the federal government from misrepresentation in a broadcasting service monopolized by the *Länder* (where, in some cases, the party in power in Bonn would be in opposition). A stronger argument was that a government might, in a crisis, need immediate and unimpeded access to the broadcasting media.

On the fringe of the debate a further idea was aired without gaining much support. The *Land*, it was suggested, was the totally wrong unit on which to base a broadcasting system; the differences in size made it impossible to ensure that all citizens would be adequately catered for technically. Broadcasting should be organized on more considered lines, dividing the area of the Federal Republic into four parts: north, west, south and south-west – plus, of course, Berlin. The only meaningful answer to this argument and to most of the points noted above continues to lie in the wholehearted support of the ARD stations for each other using existing and emerging resources, and in the unshakable priority they lend to service for the whole public of the Federal Republic.

By the time legislation had been drafted, examined by the *Bundesrat* Committee for Cultural Policy and placed before the *Bundestag* (February–March 1953), the ARD stations had given full consideration to the ideas mooted. In November 1951 the intendants had already formulated their response in a document of their own.[7] They endorsed unequivocally the sovereignty and rights of the *Länder* and of the broadcasting authorities and hinted that cases of dispute involving these rights could be referred to the Constitutional Court for adjudication. They accepted fully the necessity of making broadcasting time available to both the central and the *Land* governments on request and free of charge. The relationship to the Post Office was clarified: it would be paid for its services at a rate to be agreed between it and the broadcasting authorities, but after this all questions of finance belonged with the ARD and the individual stations. The intendants emphasized their ability to cope with this side of their affairs, particularly with the creation of a fair balance between the stations. New technical developments also fell well within the purview and

[21]

competence of the existing bodies. There was no call for new and additional institutions of control, the individual stations had their own constitutional supervisory bodies and, through the ARD, had access to the joint *Gesamtrat* in questions of wider import. As it thus resisted the proposed legislation, the ARD enhanced its own understanding of its status and function in the West German federal system.

The intendants' case was very carefully considered and found wide support, and in the face of this opposition the central government did not press for legislation when its bill eventually came before the *Bundestag*. Had it become law, the *Gesetzentwurf über die Wahrnehmung gemeinsamer Aufgaben auf dem Gebiete des Rundfunks* (bill on the accomplishment of common tasks in the field of broadcasting),[8] would have superseded all prior legislation and created a new public corporation, *Der Deutsche Rundfunk* (the German broadcasting authority). This new body would have broadcast alongside the other radio stations as the *Deutscher Gemeinschaftsrundfunk* (very roughly: German co-operative broadcasting service) and would have been supplied with material free of charge by them, except for news services and political commentaries where it would have had its own arrangements; it would also have supervised the *Deutscher Fernseh-Rundfunk* (German television broadcasting service), and long- and short-wave broadcasting, administered licensing and performed other common tasks.

This somewhat protracted first exchange set the pattern for the future rounds in the debate; it was certainly clear at this stage what the central government could usefully assume responsibility for, and where it would always be debarred. However, it did reintroduce similar legislation in 1955 (when the package made no progress) and in 1959. The latter effort brought some small gains for the central government; it also led to its defeat in the Constitutional Court.

By 1955 the Federal Republic had been granted full sovereignty (5 May 1955) and more central action was called for to compensate for the loss of allied supervision in international areas (wavelength agreements and the like). During 1954 the *Bund* and the *Länder* discussed possible broadcasting legislation and eventually a commission of experts representing the two sides drew up four draft agreements between the *Bund* and the *Länder*,[9] which were intended to secure a common standpoint on broadcasting and set up three new bodies for short-wave, long-wave and television broadcasting. While the existing situation would have been confirmed in the general agreement, the new stations would have had both *Land* and *Bund* representation on their controlling bodies. Although the central government's approach had been modified and the ARD idea for control was to be kept, the reactions of the broadcasting authorities were predictably negative: the ARD had already established itself in the fields now in contention and was unwilling to yield up anything of its territory; the broadcasters' unswerving determination to maintain their sovereign position was again demonstrated in a counter-proposal (December 1955).[10] It was seen that there were some areas where the *Bund* could usefully have a voice, such as wavelength negotiations and short-wave and long-wave broadcasting for foreign audiences, but the possibility of a compromise was not real at this time.

By this time the three groups involved in the altercation were in fairly close agreement on at least two points: the need to join forces in questions of wavelength allocations and the need for a broadcasting station representing the Federal Republic. When the issue of central legislation was reopened, the *Bund* was successful in securing the right to establish two broadcasting stations under federal law to represent the interests of the nation: *Deutsche Welle*, broadcasting on the short waveband to countries around the world, and *Deutschlandfunk*, projecting the image of Germany on the long waveband to the rest of Europe and particularly to the German Democratic Republic. The two were created in law on 29 November 1960 and effectively took over the work started by the ARD which, using the facilities of NWDR, had started broadcasting a short-wave programme for the rest of the world in 1953 and had been interested in long-wave possibilities for about the same length of time. The two draw material from the ARD stations in much the same way as had been suggested in 1953.

Although agreement was reached fairly easily in this case, where the new bodies met an obvious need and in no way infringed the rights of the existing stations (both became members of ARD), broadcasting legislation continued to be the subject of bitter exchanges. Now, however, a pitched battle was to be fought – not about a federal law on broadcasting, but about central government involvement in the development of a second television channel. The founding of DW and DLF went almost unnoticed in the mounting storm which had been brewing for at least two years and which blew itself out only in early 1961 in the chambers of the Constitutional Court.

THE CONTEST FOR THE
SECOND TELEVISION CHANNEL

The contest for the second television channel is an important chapter in the history of West German broadcasting and of West German democratic federalism. The young state was then entering its period of political storm and stress, for the television crisis was followed some 18 months later by the *Spiegel* crisis[11] and the onset of student demonstrations; a key ministerial resignation (Strauss) and eventually the end of the Adenauer government with all that this implied marked the political consequences of government interference in the media. The mood of the country was changing.

The head-on collision between the *Bund* and the *Länder* was the last act of the second channel drama. It started innocuously enough with the ARD. The ARD had been planning, well within its constitutional rights, an expansion of television services to correspond with the availability of new wavelengths in the ultra high frequency range. In May 1957 it announced that it was in a position to predict that the second channel would be ready to open in 1960. The restraining factor was the availability of wavelengths. Later in 1957 the ARD applied to the Federal Post Office for the use of the new frequencies. A somewhat delphic reply hinted that the ministry was considering other possibilities in the field. Rumours suggested that the government was exploring the feasibility of contracts with private capital to develop the second channel. In January 1958 the SPD opposition in Bonn took up the inquiry in a parliamentary question and the name *Freies Fernsehen* (Free Television) became known. An attempt was being made to wrest some sovereignty from the *Länder* and from the broadcasting authorities; the government referred the question to the Standing Committee for Cultural Affairs with the pointer: 'The objective should be *inter alia* a second programme not made by the existing broadcasting authorities.'[12]

In December 1958 the first open move by private capital came with the founding of the company *Freies Fernsehen GmbH* by an industrialist, R. Krause, acting on behalf of the Confederation of German Industry, and a newspaper publisher, H. Merkel, acting for several colleagues. The interest taken by industrialists in the commercial prospects of television and by the newspaper publishers in reducing the number of potential competitors for advertising income makes the alliance an almost predictable one and explains their willingness to help break the monopoly of the *Länder*. As yet there was no public alliance between the central government and the new company; this was to emerge a year later, after a long summer and autumn of hard debate between *Bund* and *Länder* over broadcasting legislation.

The central government's plans were discussed by the prime ministers of the *Länder* at their conference in June 1959 when they made one or two very plain statements on the subject.[13] Rejecting the proposals put forward, they concentrated on the most sensitive area, television. They declared their willingness, while upholding their sovereignty in cultural affairs and broadcasting, to negotiate their own inter-*Land* agreement authorizing the existing broadcasting bodies to create a public corporation to broadcast television (to be called *Deutsches Fernsehen*) under the control of a council made up of representatives of the *Bund*, the *Länder*, the broadcasting authorities and the public. The federal government ignored this idea and pressed ahead with the proposed legislation.

In December 1959, seeking a way of breaking the deadlock that had ensued, the federal government commissioned the *Freies Fernsehen GmbH* to start preparations for a second television programme and offered guarantees on the loan of the necessary capital (DM20m). The alliance thus created bore an uncanny resemblance to the Nazi link-up with big industry and the press; however, it was resisted for more tangible reasons. Adenauer wanted to form a joint company between the *Bund* and the *Länder* using the commercial company as a vehicle. He was supported by some of his CDU friends in the *Land* governments. There were now three competing projects in the field: the ARD proposal, the public corporation suggested by the prime ministers, and the Adenauer venture – the only one then making rapid progress. Adenauer wanted the station to open in 1961 (significantly, election year) and the *Freies Fernsehen GmbH* began to expand, founding a sister company to produce news and current affairs programmes (*Deutscher Fernsehdienst GmbH* – German Television Services). Two further companies were encouraged to put in applications for licences: in Berlin the *Berliner Tageszeitungen mbH* (Berlin Daily Newspapers) and a combine with groups in several large cities, *Vereinigte Fernsehgesellschaft GmbH* (United Television Company).

In this highly complicated situation, with his project in the balance, Adenauer broke off negotiations with the *Länder*, who were disinclined to support his proposed company; he had to act, if the 1961 deadline was to be met. In July 1960 he founded a joint *Bund-Länder* company, *Deutschland Fernsehen GmbH* (Germany Television) with DM23,000 basic capital. DM12,000 was to be the holding of the *Bund* (for which Adenauer himself signed the contract) and the other DM11,000 was to be shared equally among the 11 *Länder*; the contract was signed for the *Länder* by the Federal Minister of Justice, in the expectation that each would soon take up its holding. The *Länder* were faced with the choice of accepting this enforced participation, or of forfeiting any say in the control of the second channel. They refused to be drawn in, left the *Bund* holding all the shares and took the matter instead to the Constitutional Court. Adenauer had acted quite palpably out of a feeling of frustrated power – as he would again two years later when faced with a recalcitrant *Spiegel*.

The *Länder* charged the central government with unconstitutional behaviour. In consideration of the seriousness of this accusation, the court decided that it could not make a ruling before February 1961. Although the matter was now *sub judice*, there was nothing to stop Adenauer pressing ahead with his plans to start broadcasting over the second channel in January 1961. In October the *Länder*, led by Hamburg, realizing that they had to act quickly to prevent the creation of a *fait accompli*, asked the court to issue an interim injunction forbidding the start of broadcasting before a ruling had been given. The injunction was granted in December 1960.

DW and DLF had been founded by this time and the proposed television law yet again thrown out by the representatives of the *Länder* in the *Bundesrat*. Adenauer was left with a company that could not go on the air, no legislation on television and an impending ruling by the Constitutional Court. The scene was set for the *dénouement* of the second channel drama, with which West German broadcasting would be launched into the rich abandon of the 1960s.

THE RULING OF THE CONSTITUTIONAL COURT

The verdict of the court (28 February 1961) was full and unequivocal.[14] The federal government's action was adjudged to be unconstitutional and potentially detrimental to the wellbeing of the system on several important counts. It had assumed two things falsely: that broadcasting could be subsumed under the general heading of post and telecommunications and that it had the authority to act in cases of doubt about the division of legislative competence between *Bund* and *Länder* where the Basic Law did not offer any specific guidance. Any area of legislation that was supra-regional was not necessarily the province of the federal government. Broadcasting was properly speaking a cultural activity and therefore the prerogative of the *Länder*. Similarly broadcasting was an important medium for the formation of public opinion and should thus never be the prerogative of any single interest, be it a state or a private company; in the case in question the central government was the only body involved – it held all the shares. The state had absolutely no rights in the field of broadcasting and could not be involved even through the agency of a private company.

The judgement of the Constitutional Court is a document fundamental to democracy and broadcasting in West Germany; it warrants examination in some detail.

The difference between broadcasting and post and telecommunications is here established emphatically, and the interpretation is based on common parlance:

> In an interpretation following the natural understanding of the word and general usage, telecommunications comprise only the technical processes in the transmission of broadcast programmes.[15]

In the lengthy discussion on this point the relationship of broadcasting to telecommunications is made incontestably clear:

> Broadcasting, a medium of mass communication hardly to be underestimated in its political and cultural significance, is not part of, it is a 'user' of telecommunication installations.[16]

Thus one prop in the central government's case was declared semantically unsubstantial; the Basic Law was, in the court's view, a constitution for the people and its wording was not to be stretched in interpretation beyond the tolerance of normal usage.

The question of legislative competence was resolved most effectively by the court. The *Bund* has clear responsibilities to legislate in specific areas named in the Basic Law; it does not have any powers by default: 'In cases of doubt about *Bund* responsibility there is nothing to suggest that *Bund* competence applies.'[17] These areas are rather the province of the *Länder* and this is particularly the case with cultural phenomena: 'in so far as cultural affairs can be administered and regulated by the state ... they fall ... as fundamentally determined in the Basic Law ... in the sphere of the *Länder*.'[18] Nor can this sitution be in any way altered by the pretended need for a 'national voice' to speak in internal affairs:

> Article 30 in conjunction with articles 83ff. cannot be used to justify the production of broadcasting programmes by the *Bund* on the grounds that the production of broadcasting programmes is a 'supra-regional' task, or that the Basic Law permits the *Bund* to broadcast in the service of internal national representation and to nurture 'traditions which uphold continuity'. The *Bund* has no inherent competence for this.[19]

It is not difficult to detect in this an echo of the fear shared by the allies that centralization in broadcasting could be a first step on the road to another monopoly of German thought and life by a government or party. The court was in no doubt that state involvement in broadcasting constituted an encroachment on protected public territory:

> If the state is engaged in broadcasting in any form, then it is performing a function of public administration ... Thus, contrary to the opinion of the federal government, broadcasting as a public administrative task is included in the delimitation of competence between *Bund* and *Länder* ... and it is this even if the state, as it has done here, makes use of forms encompassed by civil law.

Throughout its commentary on the case the court underlined the basic democratic pluralism of the constitution and endorsed the vital importance of broadcasting in this framework. It did not, however, concern itself only with the public aspect of the case; as the end of the last quotation suggests, it also had something to say about private enterprise in the field of broadcasting. The company here in question was in contravention of the Basic Law:

> Article 5 precludes state control of an institution or company engaged in broadcasting ... The (*Deutschland Fernsehen GmbH*) is, however, fully in the hands of the state ... This cannot be invalidated by reference to the founding contract of the company and its standing rules ... For company law and company rules offer no guarantee against an alteration of the present form of the company.[21]

And the court was not concerned simply to condemn the device used by the federal government; its main concern was to protect the basic rights of the people through permanent laws:

> There is a fundamental difference when organizational arrangements and guiding principles designed to maintain the freedom of broadcasting are contained in a law and in a memorandum of association.[22]

However, the court did not debar all private companies from the sphere of broadcasting; in fact, it made a lengthy statement on this point which is of considerable importance for West German broadcasting, the practicalities of which have yet to be fully tested. It exists as a reminder that it is a false assumption that the *Länder* have a constitutionally protected monopoly of broadcasting:

> The guarantee of freedom in the field of broadcasting in article 5 of the Basic Law does not require, of course, the form found in the *Land* broadcasting laws and assumed by the broadcasting bodies under federal law. It is above all not a requirement of the federal constitution that broadcasting can be performed only by institutions of public law. A company incorporated under civil law could also be a vehicle for this sort of undertaking provided that it offers in its formal organization sufficient guarantees that all socially relevant groups could, as in institutions of public law, get a hearing in it and that the freedom of reporting is not infringed. Constitutionally there is no cause for misgivings about a company of this kind ...[23]

A few examples of acceptable forms are provided and the conditions are tough and dependent on supporting legislation; but the way is left open for private companies to enter broadcasting. What sort of foundation would be in a position to embark on such a venture is open to speculation. However, in these comments, two key qualities of a free public broadcasting system have been established: accessibility to all socially relevant forces and the freedom of reporting – two prerequisites that would prove an acid test for any broadcasting authority.

The court did not leave the importance of the societal groups to be divined from an *obiter dictum*; it went on to outline the way in which representation was to be effected:

> Article 5 of the Basic Law does, however, require that this modern instrument for the formation of opinion should be surrendered neither to the state nor to any one group in society. The promoters of broadcasting programmes must therefore be so organized that all relevant forces have an influence in the organs of control and a fair hearing in the overall programme, and that binding principles apply to the content of the overall programme which guarantee a minimum[24] balance in content, impartiality and mutual respect. This can be secured only if these organizational and material principles are made generally binding by law. Article 5 of the Basic Law therefore requires the enactment of such laws.[25]

This yardstick must be applied in any investigation of the West German broadcasting system, and yet even this provides no decisive criterion for the resolution of some difficult and crucial questions: what does 'have an influence' mean?; what constitutes a fair 'hearing in the overall programme'?, and what is an (acceptable) 'minimum balance in content'? – these are the indefinables in the system. Even so the court set out an ideal pattern against which all future foundations in broadcasting can be tested and which is a constant challenge for the existing stations.

Another excursus by the court, complementing its observations on fair representation, brought programme-planning within its purview. Again it is an area of fundamental relevance to the function of the mass media as informers and formers of public opinion, and again an area where the boundaries are very difficult to discern and define; the court was probing the roots of broadcasting democracy:

> Broadcasting is more than a 'medium' for the forming of public opinion; it is an eminent 'factor' in the formation of public opinion. Its contribution to the formation of public opinion is in no way limited to news broadcasts, political commentaries, series on past, present and future political problems; radio plays, musical presentations, the transmission of satirical and cabaret programmes, even programme settings help to form opinion. Every programme will have a certain tendency because of the selection and the form of the

individual transmission, particularly where a decision is involved on what is not to be broadcast, what need not interest the audience, what can be neglected without detriment to the formation of public opinion and on how what is broadcast is to be shaped and enunciated.[26]

Clearly the institutional freedom of broadcasting is as important as that of the press.

The Constitutional Court thus uncovered those difficult, often purely theoretical areas of contention that will always remain part of the mystery of broadcasting; at the same time it put an end to the federal government's efforts to establish a toehold in the sphere of broadcasting and helped the *Länder* in practice to a position of monopoly which they still enjoy. The court's ruling also contained indications of problems inherent in the West German system which did not, and do not, emanate from the central government; indeed, in part, they probably explain the latter's eagerness to be involved. These are problems of great relevance today, problems which have in recent years proved to be the acid test of democracy in the broadcasting system of the Federal Republic; problems of freedom, fairness and fullness in reporting and in overall programming; problems of excessive and unwarranted influence by individual groups.

THE FOUNDING OF ZDF

The ruling of the Constitutional Court left the federal government with no further room for manœuvre; control in broadcasting had been placed beyond its reach. The problem of opening up the second channel was seen to be the responsibility of one, or both, of the other groups involved. Of these the ARD made the first move when it resumed planning at a meeting on 14 March 1961. However, it was the *Länder* that had borne the burden of fighting the central government and they intended to occupy and exploit the territory they had conquered themselves and not present it to an intermediary agent. On 17 March 1961 the prime ministers overcame any political and particularist differences they might embody and agreed on a document that they could submit for discussion to their respective parliaments. The formula provided for a second television service broadcast from a new station independent of the structures already in existence and offering a contrast with the present programme. By 6 June 1961 an inter-*Land* agreement had been reached founding *Zweites Deutsches Fernsehen* (Second German Television). After ratification by all 11 *Länder* the agreement came into force on 1 December 1961. ZDF was located in Mainz and eventually went on the air on 1 April 1963.

Between June 1961 and April 1963 the opening which had occurred in West German broadcasting services (the second programme was wanted, the wavelengths were available, some ARD stations were technically able to exploit them) was filled at the request of the prime ministers by the ARD. This operation was more than just a service to the public, it allowed the ARD stations to look more closely at their own plans for development and provided them with an experience of value for when they started to develop third programme services.

ZDF is a public corporation and is structured administratively on parallel lines to the *Land* stations. It was, however, bound by its very nature to espouse some principles different from those of the existing stations; it serves the whole of the Federal Republic, all 11 regions together. The speed and ease with which the *Länder* arrived at a mutually acceptable arrangement reflect the unusual nature of the situation in 1961 and also, in part, the value of the decade of public debate that had preceded the moment of decision. The debate had facilitated a definition of all the requirements of the country in terms of second-channel television broadcasting and it had shown how these were not to be supplied. The ideas mooted during the debate, whatever their source, had been largely valid in terms of the structures of the broadcasting service; some were unacceptable because of the implementation proposed. The solution found by the *Länder* incorporates many of the characteristics of the central government's suggestion; to this extent ZDF represents a politically and constitutionally acceptable way of implementing plans for a central broadcasting body transmitting for home reception.

The ZDF agreement[27] has a long introductory section by comparison with the constitutions of the *Land* stations; it propounds the basic principles for the management of the station. The generally accepted tenets of truth and impartiality in reporting, of distinguishing fact from commentary and of the right of reply as well as the principle of providing access for central and regional governments on request are emphasized (§§3–6). The first paragraph of principles is, however, unusual in that it (§2) has the ring of a guideline drawn up by a central government. It shows the high degree of accord between the *Länder* at the time and their clear confidence in their ability to do democratically what they feared the central government would have done less democratically.

The station's programmes are to give television viewers in the whole of Germany an objective overall view of world events, in particular a comprehensive picture of the German reality.

These programmes are to serve above all the reunification of Germany in peace and freedom and understanding between peoples. They must be in keeping with the free, democratic basic order and facilitate the formation of independent opinion.

This paragraph shows how ZDF differs from the regional stations and from a hypothetical central government station: it is pledged to give a comprehensive picture of the whole German reality, not necessarily the forte of a regional station, and to promote, as it presents this picture, the formation of independent opinion, not necessarily a virtue in a station under central control.

It is clear that the ZDF solution is potentially better than the central government proposals; it is less clear why the *Länder* should have taken the matter out of the hands of their existing stations acting through the ARD. One simple argument would be that a new institution would bring a new approach to a situation where there was some danger of rather monochrome developments. To prevent the ARD strengthening its monopoly position was another, more political and equally valid reason why the *Länder* decided to introduce an element of competition. During the television altercation the ARD stations had put forward proposals which differed from those of the federal government and from those of the *Länder*; they had acted in a way which suggested that they thought that all sovereign rights in broadcasting rested with them. This assumption was false: they are, it is true, legally protected entities, but constitutionally the responsibility for the broadcasting services lies with the *Länder* which legislate to create the individual authorities on behalf of the public. In creating ZDF the *Länder* were adding a new variation to the system and further asserting their constitutional rights in the field – although they are an important pillar of the constitution, the broadcasting stations and (even less) the ARD do not stand in the constitutional framework on the same footing as the *Bund* and the *Länder*. Ultimately, where precisely they do stand has not yet become clear.

With the founding of ZDF the prime ministers of the *Länder* added a new and potentially valuable dimension to the West German broadcasting system. The problems of the central co-ordination of nine independent entities were eliminated and the loss of variety potentially compensated for in the improved definition of profile and the increased flexibility in internal organization. However, the circumstances of the foundation certainly justify a question about how different the ZDF service is in practice from that of the first channel and, indeed, from what the service of a government-controlled *Deutschland Fernsehen GmbH* in competition with the ARD might have been. In practice the system's potential has been undermined by the in-built financial weakness of ZDF, by bogus competition between the channels and by the inability of the political forces in the system to resist the temptation to try to dominate the single nationwide broadcasting house. A station conceived in a unique and to some extent artificial situation has proved in many ways inadequate in the uncharitable light of normalcy.

The Present West German Broadcasting System

In the West German broadcasting system there are now nine regional stations, two central radio stations (DW, DLF), one central television station (ZDF) and an American station in Berlin broadcasting in German (RIAS). The regional stations all broadcast several radio programmes, often in conjunction with each other, they share a television channel (the first programme, *Deutsches Fernsehen* – DFS) and usually have a third television channel on the air for part of the day. This very complex system is complemented by ZDF and, in a different way, by DW and DLF.

Although changes have been made in recent years in the most complicated area, the financing of broadcasting, and court rulings have added new contributions to the definition of the status of broadcasting in the West German federal state, there are still many uncertainties in the system and considerable scope for further debate and improvement. The present chapter will attempt to present a picture of the system as it functions, showing the complexity of its various interrelationships and the permanence of some of them; it is the first part of a depiction of the material structures of the system and is complemented in the following chapter which investigates the ramifications of the financial arrangements, the testing ground of the system's viability.

RIAS, DW AND DLF

RIAS stands somewhat apart from the general system and is relevant only for the sake of completeness.[1] Unlike the other

American stations which are either military or propagandist, it broadcasts in German and is an associate member of ARD; representatives of RIAS have been participating in exchanges between the various broadcasting stations since the earliest days after the war and it now (1974) makes a small contribution to the ARD budget.

RIAS was founded in November 1945 and is an institution of USIS (United States Information Service). An American supervisory body appoints the German intendant, who is then legally responsible for the running of the station. RIAS has three programmes (radio only) with the emphases in all on music (50 per cent), political commentary and news (25 per cent) and cultural commentary (10 per cent).[2] The principal significance of RIAS is political; it is a symbol of American presence in West Berlin which was of particular importance during the Berlin blockade.

DW and DLF became members of the ARD in 1962 with full voting rights in matters concerning radio broadcasting only; they are not involved in television in any way. DW broadcasts approximately two-thirds of its programmes in languages other than German (over 30 in all) and they are intended for eight principal regions in the world. It devotes only one-quarter of its time on the air to music. DW programmes are intended primarily for listeners in distant parts of the globe: the Americas, Africa, Asia, Australasia and the more distant regions of Eastern Europe – these programmes contain a minimal amount of music. The small portion of DW programmes in German thus contains a greater proportion of music. DW is only very marginally part of the home West German broadcasting system. DLF is of more importance in this respect and is in some ways comparable in status with SFB, RIAS and the morning television transmissions for viewers in the GDR. The emphasis in DLF German programmes (80 per cent of its total broadcasting time) is, however, on music (75 per cent) and cultural commentary; it moves fully into the sphere of political commentary and news for the remaining one-sixth of the time it is on the air, when it broadcasts programmes in 13 foreign (European) languages. Both these stations are the voice of Germany, DLF for Europe and DW for other continents; of the two DLF, with its particular emphasis on German culture intended to keep alive the spirit of the nation in the divided Germany, is probably the more important. Because of this role

DLF receives considerable support from the ARD, while DW is financed entirely from the federal budget. Both stations draw, as far as possible, on programmes produced by the regional stations. Both have, in 1974, contributed for the first time to the ARD budget.

THE REGIONAL RADIO PROGRAMMES

The nine ARD broadcasting houses have hitherto been called 'regional' and '*Land*' stations; there are, in fact, very few regional programmes in the strictest sense of the word. The first television programme is shared proportionally by all nine stations, but is hardly a composite of regional services. In radio broadcasting the degree of sharing and co-operation is less widely appreciated and yet there is perhaps more of it than in television. It is implemented in a different way and does not obliterate the regional nature of the programmes; it does however rob them of much of their potential individuality.

Technically radio broadcasting is not strictly regional.[3] Most areas in the Federal Republic can receive three or more VHF programmes, generally from two, but sometimes from as many as four different stations. The supply of medium-wave programmes is less good (a result of the poor postwar supply of wavelengths to Germany), but again there are few areas that can receive programmes from one station only. At night all areas can receive at least two stations, with some receiving as many as five at a tolerable level; the combined NDR/WDR medium-band programme offers viable reception in all parts of the Federal Republic. There is a high degree of pluralism in West German radio broadcasting in the sense that the individual citizen never has to rely on one station only for information and commentary.

The range of choice available to the listener would seem to be further extended by the number of programmes offered by each station. The nine stations all have two full programmes and at least an additional part programme; with their joint programme, NDR and WDR have a total of four each. The situation in practice is, however, much less varied than this would suggest; the reverse of the coin is the degree of sharing of individual items and often of part programmes. Three stations only do not yet have fixed arrangements for programme-sharing with other stations: BR, HR and RB. NDR and WDR have a common first programme;

SR co-operates in its second programme with SDR and SWF; both SDR and SWF co-operate with each other and with SR in all their three programmes; the third SFB programme was produced together with NDR until mid 1973 and SFB uses common material in all its three programmes to a greater or lesser extent each day. The selection of programmes available to the public is thus somewhat curtailed; it is further reduced by the nature of the third part-programmes which cater usually for minority interests, often for motorists on the road and foreign workers.

Radio broadcasting in the Federal Republic emerges, then, as a highly interlinked network which is differentiated in broad areas rather than into small regional units, the contrast and complement to which is the approximately 30 per cent original material broadcast by the stations. The network evolved naturally out of the co-operation started by the stations immediately after the war, and it promotes cross-fertilization at all levels. In spite of the common programmes, the programmes produced in co-operation and the loaned material, the stations have retained a strong regional flavour because the original material they produce is made up largely of news and commentary of local interest.

The main reason for the development of increasingly close ties between the stations in an apparently particularist system is economic. They cannot afford individually to produce new material all day and every day; most of them could not afford to do it for one programme only. They have combined their efforts to make the best of a situation which, with its multiplicity of stations, is inherently weak in terms of the economics of broadcasting. The vehicle the authorities gave themselves in the ARD has enabled them to develop a highly sophisticated system to exploit the resources offered by the network as a whole. The stations have not resolved their problems in this field; the economic situation is not getting better, it is expected to get worse with costs rising and *Land* governments reluctant to increase licence fees. In 1974 the willingness of the stations to increase the amount of co-operation between them is being stretched to the limit; to maintain the system the amount of 'once only' material must be cut down to an absolute minimum and all other programme material produced to a nationwide scheme and destined for a common pool – every possibility of duplication and waste of effort and resources will have to be eradicated.

[38]

The potential saving from further co-operation is foreshadowed in results already achieved (bearing in mind that it is difficult to determine the point at which further savings are made only at the cost of the system, a point some would say has been reached already); at present potential expenditure for the nine stations together is reduced by about 33 per cent.[4] The opportunities for reducing duplication are wide-ranging: a single, common evening programme from the time evening television starts, a carefully balanced common team of foreign correspondents, increased rationalization of technical installations and of their use, the development of production specialities in individual stations, are all ideas that have been suggested from time to time. All this would, in fact, be no more than an extension of the already existing pattern of co-operation, which includes virtually every aspect of radio broadcasting outside the strictly local areas of programming. It is not totally inappropriate to ponder how long it will be before the regional stations are forced to rationalize to the point of formalizing their efforts in some sort of 'national' network, throwing the basic pluralism of the system into jeopardy.

DFS

The most obvious example of co-operation in the field of television is the joint first programme, DFS. It was initiated in November 1954 by the ARD. The guidelines for it were set out in the *Verwaltungsvereinbarung über die Zusammenarbeit auf dem Gebiet des Fernsehens* (administrative agreement on co-operation in the field of television) of 27 March 1953.[5] These arrangements were properly institutionalized in a binding inter-*Land* agreement six years later (17 April 1959),[6] by which the stations were obliged to contribute to a common programme (no infringement of their rights to broadcast individual programmes is implied); they were empowered to appoint a programme director to co-ordinate their efforts, who would work with the intendants aided by a programme advisory body. The total length of the joint programme and the share of each station was to be determined by the stations in consultation through the ARD. Any station which did not produce its share of the total programme was obliged to meet the costs of the replacement.

This agreement remains the basis for the first television programme, but the stations have since produced their own revised version (1964).[7] This provides for a *Ständige Programmkonferenz* (standing programme conference) of intendants chaired by the DFS programme director, whose team in Munich prepares the ground for the meetings, and for a *Programmbeirat* (programme advisory committee). The conference plans the DFS programme on the basis of suggestions from the individual authorities who offer material for their obligatory contributions. These latter are so calculated that they effectively supplement the essential process of financial equalization between the stations. The proportions of the individual stations are:

BR	17%	RB	3%	SDR	8%
HR	8%	SR	3%	SWF	8%
NDR	20%	SFB	8%	WDR	25%

This distribution holds good for almost every area of programming, i.e. for categories of programme and for timing of programmes, so that no one station can predominate in any given field at a regular time of the viewing day or week; it also means that each station has to preserve a minimum degree of flexibility. Within this framework there is a necessary elasticity to ensure smooth functioning: any station can decide not to join the main transmission and substitute something of its own choice for the programme in question in its own region; Eurovision transmissions reduce the total programme time; some stations undertake to perform certain regular services for all the stations, again reducing the total shared time; some programmes are joint projects in which the costs are shared by all the stations in the proportions outlined above. Of the total DFS time some 40 per cent falls to programmes not included in the proportional distribution, i.e. programmes as described and repeat items; the rest is contributed in original material in the proportions given.

THE REGIONAL AND THIRD TELEVISION
PROGRAMMES

Careful co-operation and a delicately balanced budget are the key characteristics of the regional and third television programmes broadcast by the stations. The situation here reflects most strongly the situation in the radio sections of the stations: a proliferation of institutions duplicating effort and expense throughout the system.

The regional programme is broadcast over the DFS channel between the afternoon and evening sessions (18.00–20.00) and after the closedown of DFS, if required. The two hours of main viewing time contain local news, entertainment and commercial advertisements. Regional news is not a saleable commodity generally outside the region in question, so that this must remain largely an individual, costly item – NDR/RB and SDR/SWF do have joint programmes. Entertainment programmes are universally applicable, they can be and are pooled saving around 75 per cent of potential costs.[8] A complicating factor is introduced here because the authorities do not produce the commercial spots themselves, they have generally placed the task of providing these and the programme framing them in the hands of subsidiary commercial companies. These subsidiaries are independent foundations, although they work within the constitutional bounds of the stations and are owned by them. They form the subject of a separate discussion below; here it is sufficient to note that this arrangement has made the situation far from transparent. In many ways the regional programmes epitomize the greatest problems facing West German broadcasting: they need to be regional to remain viable, they have to be economically viable to be regional. In this case an attempt has been made to find a way out of this deadlock by venturing into the potentially dangerous field of commercial broadcasting.

The third programmes present a totally different picture; they are mainly regional and educational. There are five third programmes in the Federal Republic: BR, HR, WDR and NDR (in conjunction with SFB and RB) and a programme common to SR, SWF and SDR. Many of the stations have given their third programme a name which distinguishes it: BR, in 1964 the first to advance into this sphere, has a *Studienprogramm* (study programme), HR emphasizes the regional nature of its *Hessisches Fernsehprogramm* (Hessen television programme) and the joint SR/SDR/SWF programme has been given a supra-regional name with a modern ring, *Südwest 3* (south-west 3).

The third channel in television offers programmes for minority viewing, in particular for a minority with an interest in culture and education. Between 80 and 90 per cent of third-programme time is devoted to broadcasts which could be termed educational; cultural and informational programmes complement school broadcasts and other more formal courses. Bavarian third-programme broadcasting was given a very strong educational bias from the start and the *Telekolleg* (not so much a university of the air as a technical college of the air, an open technical college) was a Bavarian innovation;[9] Bavarian rather than BR because the *Land* in Germany has the responsibility for education and must, therefore, sanction and supervise the teaching of the courses and the examination schemes which lead up to recognized diplomas. This aspect of broadcasting is the only one for which *Land* financial aid (although sometimes debated) is acceptable.

Financial considerations have forced the stations to combine their efforts in the third-programme field more comprehensively even than the reduced number of programmes suggests. In August 1966, through the ARD, the stations agreed to make all appropriate third-programme material available free for three years to all stations.[10] The savings are considerable; the smaller stations are again assisted most and in an area where they would otherwise probably not function. Here the stations have also taken the next logical step in their co-operation: programme-planning is discussed by all the stations together to enable them to maximize their use of resources as a whole and individually. The educational field is one in which exchange is most readily achieved, even extending beyond national boundaries: France, Britain, Belgium and the Netherlands (as well as the other German-speaking countries) now all participate in exchanges with the German stations working through ARD. This development is of obvious significance for the future when it is foreseeable that a great variety of educational material of outstanding excellence will be commonly available throughout western Europe.

The state of education in Europe is, however, a concern for some future European government; the state of education in West Germany has been and still is a cause of great concern for politicians and educationists alike. In this context the Bavarian *Telekolleg* is of considerable importance. Bavaria long had the reputation of being the *Land* with the worst conditions in (particularly primary) education. Great efforts have been made (largely successfully) to make up this deficit; in the process a new institution has emerged whose potential value for education generally in the Federal Republic is enormous. If one leaves aside the general improvement in the educational level of the populace as people watch programmes out of interest and curiosity with no desire to gain further qualifications, if one discounts the improved social cohesion when teachers, pupils and parents can have recourse to common material to revise or supplement their knowledge – a cohesion sadly lacking in West German life – then one is left with the formal courses leading to diploma and other certificatory grades; these meet an outstanding need in West German education, opening up valuable qualifications for many members of the community who had previously been denied real educational opportunities.[11] The *Telekolleg* has brought a new dimension of democracy to West German education; it could mark a turning-point in an educational system where mobility is hardly a viable concept. The gap in the educational system, so painfully obvious when it is measured against the technical achievements of the GDR system, has always been in the higher reaches of ordinary secondary education, in the 'technical college' bridge to higher education proper.

With the spread of adaptations of the *Telekolleg* principle to other *Länder*, and with the concomitant use of common material in several *Länder*, a further interesting and important step forward in German education has been taken. The federalistic structure in education had created a virtually anarchic and disintegrative system; standards varied so completely from *Land* to *Land* that even geographical mobility was seriously impaired. Now education through the broadcasting media using standard material has brought an as yet small but nonetheless significant degree of reason and order into an otherwise chaotic picture.

It is not possible within the framework of the present work to present a full survey of developments in educational broadcasting and of their relationship to developments in educational policy at *Bund* and *Land* level; the field must await research elsewhere.

ARD AND ZDF

ZDF was established from the start as an alternative programme to ARD's DFS; it cannot, by its very nature, be a member of ARD. The two bodies are required – on the one hand by the ZDF constitution and also together by a resolution of the prime ministers (May 1962)[12] – to offer the public a better choice of viewing by providing contrasting programmes. In practice the most striking contrast has so far been found in the third channel when compared with the other two. The ZDF/ARD relationship has always been a most delicate balance in that they have not catered for different groups of viewers so much as vied for the same viewers. In 1974 the indications are that the two channels are beginning to change as they strive for better definition and contrast under the challenge from the third programmes, and in response to the demand for better services in return for licence increases.

ARD and ZDF are part of the same system, they are controlled ultimately by the same legislators, the *Länder*, and they work together constantly to serve the same public. They consult and co-operate at three principal levels: in overall programming, in the morning and early afternoon services intended for viewers in the GDR, and in some of the ARD technical work, to which ZDF can legitimately contribute.

In pursuit of the *Länder* decision, the two channels agreed on a pattern of consultation to implement the contrast;[13] a general programme structure is drawn up and reviewed at six-monthly intervals and the details of programmes are discussed at monthly meetings. The general discussions are conducted in the co-ordination committee (seven members of each body voting unanimously), while the programme directors discuss the details; additionally each delegates one representative for sport and one for Eurovision transmissions to co-ordinate these aspects of programming.

The critical point in the ARD/ZDF co-ordination is the definition and interpretation of the concept of contrast in terms relevant to the quality of the public service provided. So far the contrast has not been very meaningful, it has been a Tweedledum and Tweedledee rivalry; but ZDF is now in its second decade, the inter-*Land* agreement has been renewed and the resultant gain in ZDF confidence is promising to make the two more truly complementary. Straight competition between the two is as little a service to the public as is a lack of competition between them; the former leads to a situation where both give the public what it wants most (as measured in viewing figures), while the latter attenuates their concern for the public's wishes. There is, obviously, considerable scope within the framework of one balanced system for three channels producing three very different and complementary programmes with no danger of any becoming redundant; the situation in the Federal Republic is potentially conducive to a bold and viable solution – at least in respect of the components of the system. For the system to realize its potential the politicians who ultimately control it must liberate it from all the constraints that are inhibiting its growth.

The *Vormittagsprogramm* (the joint programme intended for viewers in the GDR) presents no problems of balance and co-ordination, since it is a composite programme established in 1966 by all the ARD stations individually and ZDF;[14] it stands quite apart from the programme co-ordination of ZDF and ARD as a body. There is a properly constituted production department (*Redaktion Vormittagsprogramm ARD/ZDF*) and all administration[15] carried out by SFB as the broadcasting station most concerned with the actual transmission of the programmes. NDR transmitters are also used, along with those of HR and BR closest to the GDR border. The programme is broadcast daily from 10.00 until 13.30 (until 10.50 on Sundays) and the material is provided free by ARD and ZDF in roughly equal quantities; the ARD portion is shared by the nine stations in their agreed (DFS) ratio. As in the DFS agreement the stations are obliged to provide their share, or bear the cost of the substitution. All centrally incurred expenses are met by the stations on the same basis as their general arrangement for financial balance.

In its own way the 'a.m. programme' functions as a television *Deutschlandfunk* although it has, by the very nature of the medium, a more narrowly circumscribed range. Its programmes consist mainly of repeats from ARD and ZDF programmes, but can be adapted to give live coverage of events of particular significance in inter-German relations. It is clearly open to debate whether the changing relations between the two Germanies and the increasing financial difficulties of the broadcasting system will allow the programme to continue with its status unchanged; it could soon become altogether anomalous, an expensive and embarrassing luxury. It could also reveal itself as the pioneer of morning television broadcasting within the Federal Republic, adding a fourth dimension to the television system.

The third aspect of ARD/ZDF co-operation lies in the technical field, where developments are of importance to all broadcasting bodies equally and have no implications for programme policies. In these areas of common interest, where economies can be made by increasing participation, the ZDF contribution to ARD work is welcome and profitable. ZDF makes a regular contribution to the two ARD technical institutions: *Das Institut für Rundfunktechnik GmbH* (institute for broadcasting technology), a research body, and the parallel teaching body, *Schule für Rundfunktechnik*; it is also represented on the occasional (joint) commission, e.g. for the Olympic Games.

The ZDF agreement was renewed by the *Länder* with effect from 1 January 1971; the basic system will continue for some time to come in its present form. The economic weaknesses of the system are forcing both ARD and ZDF to look closely at its shortcomings, bringing them together as allies in a common cause and increasing the prospects of improvement in the public service offered. The balance between the two is not stable, as indeed the balance in broadcasting generally is not; it will have to be adjusted to meet the needs of broadcasting in the European Germany of the 1980s when the narrow federalism out of which the present system grew will, perhaps, have become totally inappropriate.

THE ARD COMMITTEES

In a system in which the broadcasting authorities are becoming increasingly interdependent in all aspects of their work, the activities of their associative organization has become increasingly diversified and professionalized. The ARD is empowered by §5(7) of its statute to create various bodies to explore specific areas and, in some cases, to keep them constantly under review. The ARD committee structure, its *Kommissionen*, is virtually self-explanatory; the *Kommissionen* are a cross between working parties and standing committees with certain powers of decision which enable them to promote effective co-ordination in the areas under their purview without adding to the burden of the main ARD assembly.

One of the more important bodies which is part of the committee structure, the DFS *Ständige Programmkonferenz*, has been discussed already and another, the *Finanzausgleichsgremium* – in essence a special committee – is discussed below. The four standing committees proper, each of which has its own sub-committees, are the *Finanzkommission* (finance), the *Hörfunk-programmkommission* (radio programmes), the *Juristische Kommission* (legal) and the *Technische Kommission* (technical). The members of these four important bodies are the heads of the relevant sections in the individual stations: the administrative directors (finance), the directors of radio programmes, the legal advisers and the technical directors. The intendants themselves sit on the DFS programming body and are, as the decision-makers of the ARD, the group to whom the committees report. In spite of the coincidence of membership, which gives the *Ständige Programm-konferenz* a standing almost parallel to the ARD working assembly, it is essentially a standing committee with sub-groups similar to those of the other standing committees; in this case the chairmen of these sub-committees (here called *Kommissionen*) are usually the programme directors for television from the stations.

The *Sonderkommissionen* (special committees) resemble *ad hoc* working parties and differ greatly in their degree of importance and permanence. They can be formed to meet a specific situation (a special event), or they can be given special responsibility for a difficult area of importance which would not be covered in the normal terms of reference of any one of the main committees (for example, relations with the Federal Post Office). There are usually some 12 of these special committees looking into spheres as different as the maintenance of an efficient network of foreign correspondents and the promotion of Franco-German friendship, satellite communication and media research, educational broadcasting and common investment policies – to mention some of them. The significant feature here is that in nearly every case the chairman is an intendant.

As the responsibility for the management of ARD administration rotates with the chairmanship from station to station, so the chairmanship of the four standing committees follows suit – an obvious aid to administrative co-ordination as well as a fair sharing out of the burdens involved. The chairmanship of the other committees is usually for the life of the committee and usually falls to someone with a particular interest in its allotted task. In this way the intendants develop certain specialisms which add depth and balance to their work as a group. The fact that the intendants head these committees has, however, significance of a different kind in the context of the German broadcasting system. The various committees are all designed to facilitate the work of the ARD and although they cannot take final decisions themselves, they can act within discretionary limits. The intendants, who are the decision-makers, acquire a certain representative role as chairmen of the various committees – they become indirectly representative of the whole system. Their position is strengthened further by the system of open representation that forms another facet of the work of the ARD.

The ARD delegates representatives to sit on various international bodies as well as on committees of organizations within the Federal Republic. The *Deutscher Bühnenverein* (association of German theatre directors), for example, has two ARD representatives on its committees, while in the international field the ARD is strongly represented – in the general assembly and in the special commissions of the EBU, for example. Again the intendants figure largely in the lists of representatives, supported appropriately by the technical and programme directors and by the legal advisers.

Thus the ARD can be seen in the light of its committee and representative structures as a small team of professional broadcasters working together to solve common problems. The team is made up of the senior administrators of the stations and is led by the small nucleus of 12 intendants, of whom three are of very minor significance. The intendants take all decisions of importance in the ARD and are heads of their own stations; they are demonstrably the key figures in the broadcasting system. They can do much to guide and protect it in the maelstrom of influences to which it is open. Through their actions – or lack of action – they can also surrender broadcasting to forces not wholly identified with the ideals of public service. The pressures on the system are varied and powerful; to cope with them the intendants need all the corporate strength of the ARD. The resistance of the system to the forces of the world outside is not least a factor of the cohesion of the structures created in the ARD and of the identity of purpose it has engendered in its members.

The Financing of the West German Broadcasting System

THE BASIC SYSTEM

The arrangements for financing broadcasting in West Germany are extremely complex and are currently in a state of flux. After a decade and a half of stability and prosperity, the late 1960s and early 1970s have brought considerable movement into the system with two changes in the licence fees payable by radio and television owners, a reorientation in the attitude of the Federal Post Office to the charges it is entitled to make for its services, and two taxation cases contested before the highest courts by ZDF and ARD.

Paradoxically the changes made in fees, which may prove to be the first steps in a policy of regular adaptations to the changing economic and social climate, have been accompanied by and are in part the result of increasing transparency in a situation hitherto shrouded in unwarranted secrecy. While ZDF has produced a statement of its work every year since the opening of the station (the first account came in 1965 for the years 1962–64), the ARD stations guarded their activities from the eye of the general public in varying degrees until 1969 when the first ARD yearbook was published. Since 1971 (with statistics for 1970), this latter has included statements of account for the ARD and for the individual stations in standardized form, thus allowing some comparison. Since 1971 the statistics have been comprehensive, offering a new and welcome dimension of openness.

The move away from secrecy was dictated in the final analysis by necessity: the prime ministers, in granting the broadcasting authorities more income through increased licence fees (implemented 1970), insisted that the stations make their financial situation more accessible and the stations have, for their part, seen the wisdom of explaining to their public why they need more money. The second licence increase (January 1974) was given very full coverage in the press when the prime ministers approved it in July 1973. The West German public needed to be told the background to the extra financial demands to be made on it. It remains to be seen whether it now appreciates something of this very complex system: the longstanding arrangements between the ARD stations, the peculiar status of ZDF, the ambiguous nature of the stations' commercial earnings and the as yet only partially clarified taxation status of public broadcasting. The system is difficult because it has evolved organically, it was not drafted on a drawing-board, and it is significant that the drawing-board station, ZDF, is the one facing the most acute difficulties and uncertainties.

There are two main sources of income in West German broadcasting: the income from the public in the form of licence dues, and the income from commercial advertising. The latter is discussed separately below.

The latest developments in licensing have effectively created a unified system for all the *Länder*. Fees have always been the same in all *Länder*, but now so also are the rules about exemptions and reductions for social and other reasons. The stations are now also obliged to act in unity in the administration of their public moneys. However, the application of one set of rules to 11 fundamentally different *Länder* and nine even more different broadcasting stations does not serve to equal out these differences; it aggravates any discrepancies and only emphasizes further the economic imbalance in the system. (Table 1 reveals the vast differences in the number of licences payable in each of the nine areas.) Increased licence fees cannot, in themselves, provide a solution to the basic problems of the system, in which inequality has been an inherent characteristic – it was one reason why the central government wanted to legislate federally and introduce a degree of rationality in the 1950s. To give themselves a firmer basis for their resistance to government moves in other areas, the stations and the *Länder* responded to the financial challenge by themselves modifying the system. The mechanisms devised were ingenious and they seemed to work well during the prosperous 1960s; the changed economic climate has now begun to show up the weaknesses of the system and finance has again emerged as a priority problem.

Table 1. Radio and television licence-holders in the areas served by the nine regional stations

1 April 1974	Radio Licences			Television Licences		
	Paying	Free	Total	Paying	Free	Total
BR	3,284,657	179,668 (5·2%)	3,464,325	2,887,208	158,352 (5·2%)	3,045,560
HR	1,762,716	118,724 (6·3%)	1,881,440	1,594,318	104,234 (6·1%)	1,698,552
NDR	3,641,306	290,726 (7·4%)	3,932,032	3,351,829	264,026 (7·3%)	3,615,855
RB	257,940	17,400 (6·3%)	275,340	236,134	15,914 (6·3%)	252,048
SR	341,043	10,434 (3·0%)	351,477	316,664	9,696 (3·0%)	326,360
SFB	881,985	70,491 (7·4%)	952,476	786,511	60,796 (7·2%)	847,307
SDR	1,887,838	95,380 (4·8%)	1,983,218	1,570,160	74,819 (4·5%)	1,644,979
SWF	2,210,628	129,029 (5·5%)	2,339,657	1,924,836	109,883 (5·4%)	2,034,719
WDR	5,099,608	427,898 (7·7%)	5,527,506	4,774,639	397,656 (7·7%)	5,172,295
Total	19,367,721	1,339,750 (6·5%)	20,707,471	17,442,299	1,195,376 (6·4%)	18,637,675

(Source: *Media Perspektiven*, 4/1974, 181.)

Until 1968 the status of the licence fee itself was only inadequately defined. Rulings by the Federal Administrative Court (*Bundesverwaltungsgericht*, 15 March 1968) and the Federal Constitutional Court (27 July 1971)[1] have helped to clarify the situation considerably. The broadcasting authorities were only indirectly involved in the 1968 case, when the Federal Post Office was accused by a claimant in Bavaria of unlawfully refusing an exemption from licence fees. *Inter alia* the court elucidated the relative rights and authority in relation to licence fees of Post Office, broadcasting authority and *Land*. The Post Office is merely an instrument employed by the broadcasting stations to collect fees and perform other tasks appropriate to it; fees are determined by the *Länder*, which have sole rights in this as in all aspects of broadcasting – they also determine the qualifications for exemption; the fees are payable to the broadcasting authorities for whose sole use they are intended, a use which includes the payment of the Federal Post Office for its services.

In practice this ruling proved to be double-edged; it caused both Post Office and *Länder* to face the newly established facts of the situation. The *Länder* legislated[2] to increase licence fees and standardize exemptions (they also demanded a new approach by the stations); the Post Office decided that it would be paid in future for the actual services rendered and not by way of an agreed regular contribution from each licence paid, to which it had no legal right. These were some of the facts the system had previously been able to ignore; facing them brought the stations not a net gain but a potential overall loss – the extra demands on the system more than offset the extra income.

The facts of financing the West German broadcasting system are often misrepresented. Licences are dual: there is a basic licence and a combined licence. The basic licence entitles the holder to receive radio programmes, but the fee paid is a *Grundgebühr* (basic due) or *Rundfunkgebühr* (broadcasting due) and not, as is often erroneously assumed, a *Hörfunkgebühr* (radio due). The combined licence is often seen as a radio licence plus a television licence, but as the holder has to pay the full amount whether he owns a radio or not, it is properly speaking a basic licence plus a supplementary television licence. There is as yet no extra charge for colour reception.

Since 1 January 1974 the combined licence has cost DM10.50 per month (roughly £21 per annum) which comprises a basic due of DM3 and a television supplement of DM7.50. These new rates mark an increase of DM0.50 and DM1.50 respectively over the levels agreed by the *Länder* for 1 January 1970, the increase now being exactly 50 per cent when measured in terms of the previous longstanding rates of DM2 and DM5. It must be emphasized that the change implemented in 1970 was the first increase in the postwar period; it was in fact the first actual increase in broadcasting dues in Germany since 1924.

The first increase was a surprisingly long time in coming – partly because of the reluctance of the *Länder* to agree to it and partly because it was only in the mid 1960s that the general increase in the number of radio and television sets in the Federal Republic slowed to a point where the annual increment from additional licences became insufficient to meet the increased needs of the stations. Ownership of radio and television sets in the Federal Republic has now reached virtual saturation point, the figures having stagnated since early 1974 (some 91·6 per cent of all households hold a basic licence and some 82·4 per cent a television supplement);[3] meaningful increases in income are possible now only if licence dues are increased or if new supplements are introduced for colour or stereophonic reception, for example.

The *Land* parliaments overcame their reluctance to raise fees when the competence for this had been firmly ascribed to them and when they had devised a face-saving set of accompanying changes that would enable them to uphold the prestigious image of a cheap system. The improvements they required of the stations, allied with the extension of licence exemptions, the increased demands of the Post Office and predictable increases in running costs, forced the stations to ask almost immediately for the second increase. This was an important step and introduced a significant new factor: an unprecedented unanimity between ZDF and ARD.

Independently during the course of 1972 both ARD and ZDF arrived at the conclusion that an additional increase would be necessary by the beginning of 1974. The two bodies had been forced to improve their co-operation as part of the 1970 package; they had developed a new awareness of their financial circumstances and in this new, critical situation they presented a united front to try to impress on their common political masters the urgency of their need. In February 1973 the then ARD chairman (SWF intendant Hammerschmidt) and ZDF intendant Holzamer sent a joint letter[4] to all members of the federal and *Land* parliaments stating their case for an amelioration of the financial basis of broadcasting. They suggested that a further increase in fees to a

[53]

total of DM12 per month (DM3.50 plus DM8.50) would be required to meet the deficit expected in 1975: DM1, 000m for the ARD and DM300m for ZDF. In documenting their case they drew attention to two factors in particular which contributed (and still contribute) to their worsening situation and which lie directly under the control of the politicians: Federal Post Office charges controlled by the *Bund*, licence exemptions controlled by the *Länder*. They argued that Post Office charges already accounted for about one-third of their gross annual income and that this must become much greater in the near future. In 1970 'free licences' deprived them of a potential income of approximately DM75m, a figure that would be increased by a further DM43.5m per annum as a result of the latest amendment to the inter-*Land* agreement (1 January 1973).[5] The demands made by the broadcasters were thus considerably greater than the increase subsequently allowed.

The new rate has been fixed for a period of at least two years, which allows the prospect of a review probably in 1976, which will be roughly in step with a four-year cycle of licence increases, by which time the stations (certainly ZDF) can be expected to be in serious financial straits. It would not be totally unreal to expect a comprehensive review of the financing of broadcasting in 1977 – a year when no elections of importance are likely to be held. It is possible that the present system is in its final phase.

EQUALIZATION

Whatever happens by way of change in the late 1970s, the question of equalization between the stations, which range in size from WDR with some 5m paying licence holders to RB with 0.25m, will remain crucial – unless changes in broadcasting are accompanied or even superseded by political and administrative changes which modernize the present federal and *Land* structures. We must expect that equalization will remain a problem for the broadcasting authorities acting within the legal framework created for them by the *Länder*.

Under the present system the licence fees are collected by the Federal Post Office on behalf of the broadcasting authorities (they intend to take over this task themselves from the beginning of 1976) and an initial division is made between radio and television dues; the Post Office receives the payments due to it from each. The net television total is then divided up between ZDF and the ARD station to give ZDF its portion of 30 per cent. All this is carried out according to a predetermined formula; in 1971, for example, the DM6 television supplement was divided up to give the Post Office DM1.40, ZDF DM1.38 and ARD DM3.22.[6] The net income of the ARD stations is the basis for their code for the equalization of financial burdens (*Finanzausgleich*).

The first agreement on equalization was reached by the ARD stations in December 1958 and given binding endorsement by the *Länder* in April the following year. In 1962 a modified scheme[7] was drawn up in the light of experience and this remained the basis for the system until the licence changes were introduced in 1970 and 1974. The present agreement between the broadcasting stations was concluded on 11 September 1973.[8]

The first agreement included very complex formulae for the correct calculation of the amounts needed to introduce viable equality between the donor and the recipient stations. In 1962 the formulae were replaced by fixed proportions and the system settled to a period of stability until the ARD took some responsibility for the financing of DLF in 1968; the three recipient stations (RB, SFB, SR) began making a small contribution for this purpose. By 1969 the total budget had reached DM59.9m (from DM20m in 1960). In 1970, in an attempt to create extra flexibility as a counter to the increased disparities which had resulted from the increase in licence fees, the stations again resorted to extremely complex formulae. In practice this method seemed to disadvantage the medium-sized stations and the 1973 system shows a return to fixed amounts; it can be seen as drawing together the threads of all earlier experience – if it is not successful, the system will be shown to have reached the point where only outside help can guarantee its future.

The equalization fund is administered by a committee (*Finanz-ausgleichsgremium*) on which all ARD stations are now represented (including DW, DLF and RIAS, which now make small contributions to the budget) and in which the three main donor stations (WDR, NDR, BR) have three votes each and the rest one each. The financial obligations of the stations are set out definitively in the agreement, so that the commitments to provide ARD programme material, for example, are already included in the

individual totals which make up the annual fund of DM116.55m.
The breakdown of the fund shows the following contributions:

BR	16.24m	SDR	4.80m
HR	5.60m	SWF	6.25m
NDR	24.28m	WDR	54.50m
RB	0.71m	DW	0.36m
SR	0.90m	DLF	0.36m
SFB	2.37m	RIAS	0.18m

The fund is expended in the following way:

common tasks	18.00m	SR	20.16m
DLF	33.60m	RB	16.45m
SFB	28.34m		

The equalization agreement now includes all the West German
stations except ZDF and has clearly placed the burden of the
system on the three large stations. The fact that RIAS and, in
particular, DW have been included as donors can be interpreted in
two ways: as a sign of the desperate financial situation of broadcasting and as proof of increasing solidarity between all the
broadcasting authorities. The principle on which the equalization
arrangement was founded was the promotion of broadcasting on
a nationwide basis, i.e. so that none of the stations would cease to
function. So far the system has been successful, but the scraping of
pittances from stations with no licence income and the absolute
dependence (ultimately) on one large station (in a *Land* where
politicians often threaten to withdraw from the system) are not
good omens for the future. The situation in the mid 1970s seems
to portend one course of action – a thorough revision of the
financial bases of the system and with it inevitably of the foundations of public broadcasting in a pluralistic framework.

THE COMMERCIAL SIDE OF THE ARD STATIONS

The financial difficulties created by the stagnation of licence
income with rising costs and the deterioration of the balance
between the stations have caused speculation about the closure of
the smaller stations and about the spread of commercial exploitation. The latter is an interesting question because the point at issue
is less the founding of commercial stations than the increased

importance of commercial income to the public broadcasting authorities. The problems of ARD and ZDF are quite different in this respect. ZDF relies very heavily on income from commercial advertising to supplement its income from licences and the commercial programme is controlled by a department within the station. In the ARD stations the system is much more complex: these draw most of their income from licences (both radio and television) and supplement this only modestly from commercial income; they do not have internal departments controlling the commercial side of their broadcasts but entrust this function to subsidiary companies. The different role of commercial income in the two cases is easily illustrated:[9] in 1971 ARD net income (radio and television) from advertising was DM117.6m and the net revenue from licences DM1, 118.4m; in the same year ZDF commercial income yielded a net return of DM234.3m, while licence dues brought in only DM257m.

The importance of ARD commercial income is different for radio and for television; the 1971 figures again give a generally valid perspective:

	DM
Net income from radio licences (all stations)	480.5m
Net income from radio commercials (all stations)	30.9m
Net income from television licences (all stations)	637.8m
Net income from television commercials (all stations)	86.7m

Thus commercial income in radio is about 6 per cent of the total from both sources and in television about 12 per cent of the total. The difference arises partly because the two largest stations (WDR, NDR) do not permit commercial advertising on their radio channels.

For the ARD stations, then, commercial sources provide merely a useful supplementary income; if there is any commercial threat to the public control of broadcasting it is in individual stations and in their radio programmes. An outline of the system will show how.

Advertising on television (DFS and ZDF) is restricted to a daily average over the year of 20 minutes (Sundays and national holidays are kept free of commercials) broadcast between 18.00 and 20.00, the time set aside in the ARD programme for the regions. The maximum time allowed for commercial insertions in any one day is 25 minutes. In radio the situation varies from station to station; WDR and NDR have no commercials and most stations restrict their inclusion to morning and early afternoon programmes and to specific channels. There is a tendency for commercial advertising to spread, particularly into the programmes intended for motorists (usually the third programmes during the day). As yet no sponsoring of programmes is allowed, but time can be purchased in some stations on the understanding that all the insertions it will carry will be made in the course of a selected programme. This already leads to some diffusion of commercial influence into the surrounding programme. Although BR has been the postwar leader in the field, introducing radio commercials on 16 September 1949 and television commercials on 3 November 1956, SR has the reputation of being the most commercialized ARD station.[10]

There is some cause for concern over television commercials, but it is not, as in radio, that the programme framing the commercial spots is used for sneak advertising, it is rather that these *Rahmenprogramme* have tended to exploit cheap material. The problem is easily pinpointed: there is straight competition between ARD and ZDF during the period when the commercials are broadcast (not part of the ARD/ZDF co-ordination agreement) and popular material is used to draw viewers from the rival channel. It does seem, however, that this situation is ripe for change; ZDF has begun (1973) to experiment in this programme area and the need for improvement is generally accepted within the ARD.

Change in the ARD stations is less easy than in ZDF, because the commercial side of their programmes is divorced from the main business of the stations and placed in the hands of subsidiary commercial companies. Each company has quite independent status within its station, although it does work within the latter's constitutional rules. The station authorities are often consulted and the intendant, of course, must retain overall control of and responsibility for what is broadcast, but each subsidiary has its own financial structure and must strive to maximize profits. The framework programme, for which the subsidiary is responsible administratively, is used to draw a maximum number of viewers for the commercial insertions.

The charges made for commercial spots are calculated according to the number of consumer contacts (viewers) expected and are adjusted in terms of the actual numbers. In the ARD stations these prices vary from station to station, and in the second channel they vary from month to month. ZDF initiated its system of grading charges in terms of months in 1973, taking into account the fact that viewing habits vary over the year. The ARD stations do not yet do this but they introduce a degree of flexibility by exploiting the maximum commercial time permitted (25 minutes) in the best months and by compensating to preserve the yearly average of 20 minutes per day during the poorer viewing months (summer). The standard measuring unit used by the commercial world is one thousand consumer contacts and in television advertising this is related to a spot of 30 seconds; what matters to the client is the price per thousand viewers per 30 seconds (*Tausenderpreis*). An indication of what this means in practice can be obtained from the figures for March 1973.[11] In that month the actual costs to the customer for 30 seconds of advertising time ranged from DM2,000 in SR, through DM16,200 in WDR, reaching DM32,400 in ZDF. Reviewed in terms of the *Tausenderpreis* these costs become: SR DM25.32, WDR DM11.40, ZDF DM7.49. In terms of the *Tausenderpreis*, 30 seconds of SR time was by far the most expensive in the system; BR was cheapest at DM6.25.

There are eight registered subsidiary commercial companies in the West German broadcasting system controlling seven regional commercial television programmes (some control both radio and television commercial business); NDR and RB have a common company and the SDR and SWF companies produce a common programme. Although the companies are independent, they share the essential ARD characteristic of working closely together in the interests of the system.

The demand for television commercial time was small to begin with, but by 1959 it had reached sufficient proportions for the stations, which had previously more or less shared one programme, to offer time independently of each other. While the resultant increase in the number of commercial programmes brought some relief for the commercial world, it brought obvious problems for the television subsidiary companies; there were now seven independent programmes to be made to frame the commercials. The subsidiaries saw the wisdom of continuing something of the combined operation they had enjoyed up to the end of 1959, and they also benefited from the example of the new DFS programme co-operation (institutionalized in the agreement of 17 April 1959); with effect from 1 January 1960 they decided to form a programme pool to which they would contribute in proportion to their size, each one making its contribution in terms of productions, commissions and foreign films.[12] The original size of the pool was 350 items with the number of foreign films restricted to a maximum of 120 – a measure intended to ensure that the companies did not opt constantly for cheap material (in both senses of the word). This pool of 350 items was designed to meet the demands of all the subsidiary companies, which broadcast some 300 commercial programmes each per year, and to allow some flexibility. Each company was pledged to provide material on the understanding that it would be available to all the other companies for a period of three years free of any further licence or royalty commitments. The composition and management of the pool are supervised by the Programme Commission for Commercial Television (*Programmkommission Werbefernsehen*), a composite body with one representative for each commercial company and one for each of the broadcasting authorities; the latter provide a useful filter early in the process of programming.

When the agreement was first made in 1960 there were six commercial programmes involved (SR joined later) so that the amount of material needed for all programmes, which would have totalled some 1,800 units in a year, was cut almost to one-sixth. The framing programmes have since been subdivided to permit the inclusion of an increased number of commercial spots. In 1973 the pool was increased to 450 items, which should extend the possibilities of making savings beyond the earlier estimate of DM70m annually.[13]

The significance of economies of the scale of DM70m per year is easily illustrated: in 1971 the total returns from commercials were DM478.5m which yielded a profit before taxation and before charitable donations had been made of DM200.6m and an eventual net profit of DM86.7m; without the pool the sum might have been very small indeed.[14]

It is difficult at the present time to offer any comment on the trend in commercial income. Certainly the turnover in broadcasting is less than one-quarter of the total for advertising in the publishing media and less than one-third of that of the press.[15] What is not clear is the future of commercials in radio and television. Demand for time in the former has begun to revive and the general financial situation in broadcasting could prompt WDR and NDR to drop their embargo in at least part of their programmes. In television demand exceeds by far the time available, but the outcome of the ZDF taxation case (see below) will have consequences for the ARD stations as well – they are almost certain to have to take a considerable cut in profits. In this event what is already a quite modest supplementary income could be reduced to the point of insignificance; on the other hand, faced with no hope of an increase in licence income and a need to meet pent-up taxation demands as well as rising costs, the stations could be forced to compensate for the strictly limited time they are allowed to use for commercials in television by freeing every possible minute of radio time to the commercial world. The scope here for speculation is so great as to make any prognostications of future developments meaningless.

THE FINANCING OF ZDF

In the ZDF Yearbook 1972, Ernst W. Fuhr, ZDF legal adviser, finishes a notable article on the taxableness of ZDF commercial income[16] with a short summary of the most serious aspect of the present ZDF financial situation. If the station had to meet the demands of the fiscal authorities it would be unable to produce the full programme required of it by the *Länder*, and this leaves out of account any taxation debt accumulated in the past. Looking to the immediate future Fuhr says:

> If ZDF should be defeated in the Federal Finance Court, then in this situation it would have no alternative than, invoking the constitutional guarantee of its ability to function, to approach the *Länder* with the demand that the financial foundations of broadcasting freedom be secured by a modification of §23 of the inter-*Land* agreement or in some other appropriate way.[17]

ZDF is indeed in a precarious financial situation; the amount claimed by the fiscal authorities up to the end of 1973 was already in excess of DM500m and each year's delay in reaching a settlement is adding at least DM60m to the total.[18] The problem is, however, not new, for the ZDF financial position has never been really secure; the weakness lies in the crucial §23 of the ZDF agreement:

(1) As from 1 January 1962 the station receives thirty per cent of the yield in television dues in the area of the contracting *Länder*, in so far as they have it at their disposal. The prime ministers of the contracting *Länder* are empowered to change the proportion of licence dues in a new agreement ...
(2) For the rest the station covers[19] its expenses by revenue from commercial programmes.
(3) In so far as the station has surpluses after deducting its own expenses and the necessary reserves, corresponding refunds are made out of the revenue from commercial programmes to the contracting *Länder* in relation to the number of television licence holders at the time. They are to be used for cultural purposes.

This paragraph of the agreement has caused many commentators to note simply that ZDF is financed partly from licence dues and partly from commercial income – an inadequate comment given the complexity of the situation or series of situations facing ZDF. The station's difficulties in 1973–74 may be of a different nature from those of 1963, but they arise out of the same shortcomings in the agreement. ZDF has been in some kind of financial difficulty for most of the decade of its active existence; it is time, as Fuhr has suggested, for a new look at the system.

The first ZDF yearbook, reviewing the first two years and nine months of the station's work, emphasized the unsatisfactory nature of the financial basis:

In the first place the financial basis is in no way sufficient. And the question remains, whether in the long term a more appropriate apportionment of dues between ARD and ZDF can be avoided.[20]

The difficulties at that time had arisen on three counts: ZDF had been unable to start transmission until April 1963 and had had to ask the ARD stations to fill the gap, diverting 50 per cent of its licence income to them for the service; for some months after it commenced transmission (until October 1963) it was unable to broadcast its commercial programme in the highly populous North Rhine-Westphalia and had to make considerable refunds to its commercial clients; BR contested the legality of the inter-*Land* agreement as an internal Bavarian law and refused to surrender the requisite 30 per cent of its television licence dues to ZDF until it lost the ensuing court case in November 1965.

In 1963 ZDF drew its first revenue from commercial advertising, made a loss on the year – and received its first demands for *Körperschaftssteuer* and *Gewerbesteuer* (corporation tax and trade tax). This dispute, which has been going on ever since and where a preliminary ruling indicates a decision against ZDF,[21] is over the fiscal status of ZDF commercial income. ZDF claims that §23 of the inter-*Land* agreement obligates it to draw income from commercial advertising to supplement its income from licences, making the former a substitute for and in every way comparable with the latter, i.e. not susceptible to the imposition of taxes. The ZDF argument is supported most often by reference to the intentions of the prime ministers of the *Länder* when they founded ZDF, who, there can be no doubt, wanted the station to receive its full income from commercials to enable it to fulfil the tasks laid upon it and as a guarantee of its independence. They probably also wanted to avoid increasing the load on the television licence holders at a time when they had just deprived them of a fully commercial service (*Deutschland Fernsehen GmbH*) and possibly even to make a small profit for the *Länder* (§23(3)). Whatever the intentions of the prime ministers at the time, the various finance courts which have examined the case so far have failed to see an obligation in the wording of §23; ZDF is the victim of a semantic quibble over the force of a simple present tense, which the courts believe is permissive. Because this is the issue, it has never become clear whether a straight imperative from the prime ministers of the *Länder* would carry any more weight with the federal fiscal authorities.

Although the intentions of the prime ministers can make no impression on German legal machinery, they are meaningful in the only context where ultimately a constructive solution can be found – in the political arena. The taxes in question are the subject of concurrent legislation between *Bund* and *Länder*[22] and it is doubtful whether an inter-*Land* agreement (which excludes the *Bund*) can have any binding power over the federal taxation authorities. The problem will have to be resolved now by a new definition of the ZDF financial status on which all parties, including the federal taxation authorities, agree.

A new agreement would resolve the question of principle, but there is a second interesting aspect to the ZDF taxation case which is of almost equal importance: the level at which taxation has been set and will probably be endorsed by the Federal Finance Court. The fiscal authorities have set their levy in relation to the whole of the station's commercial income, allowing a counter claim for expenditure only in relation to the commercial programme (the ARD parallel would be the commercial spots but not, as hitherto, the framework programme). ZDF is thus subject to tax on 50 per cent of its income which the taxation authorities regard as profit from one small sector of its activities; a fully commercial enterprise would have been taxed on overall net profit only – in the case of ZDF nil since it is non-profit-making. ZDF is caught in the unenviable position of being a public corporation with a small commercial section on which it has to rely to survive; the two activities are regarded in isolation one from the other by the law, the fact of public control cannot gain exemption for the commercial sector from taxation – and the latter's profits cannot be offset by the former's losses. Since ZDF income in the past has been such that it has been unable to build any reserves against the possibility of losing the case, it will soon be technically bankrupt. Apart from the political solution and a new constitution, the only possibility for ZDF would be an appeal to the Constitutional Court on the grounds that taxation on this scale by the *Bund* constitutes an infringement of the freedom of broadcasting, which includes its economic independence. By implication it could be claimed that the freedom of the *Länder* is also infringed.

A ruling against ZDF will, perhaps, be something of a *coup de grâce*; a political solution to its problems will have to be found sooner or later, for ZDF is an anomaly – an interim solution that has become too permanent. It is caught in a cleft stick which cannot be eased too soon. Like all broadcasting bodies, it has no control over its income; it cannot influence its income from licence fees which can only rise if the number of television owners rises – or if the *Länder* agree to raise either the licence fee or the ZDF portion of it – nor can it influence substantially its income from commercials which are not allowed to exceed the 20 minutes per day average and whose unit price is bound by the economics of the market.

With the calculations that led the prime ministers to sanction the 1974 licence increase, ZDF submitted a prediction (based, incidentally, on the greater increase requested by the broadcasters) that it expected to have to appeal to the *Länder* for a further review of the situation as early as 1976.[23] It seems highly likely, therefore, that the prime ministers have merely deferred a more thorough-going examination of the situation until a more convenient time, possibly when the full implications of the taxation case for all the stations, ZDF and ARD, have become apparent, and when the latter have had time to exhaust all possibilities of making further economies themselves.

ZDF has existed on a provisional footing for over a decade now and is at last beginning to shake off the psychological trammels of uncertainty; now only the financial doubt constitutes a serious factor of inhibition. Removing this is a task for the prime ministers in the *Länder* and for the political forces generally in the Federal Republic; they are in a position to take an important step forward for the whole system. Out of the present financial crisis a new ZDF could emerge which is capable of fulfilling all the promise of 1961; if the political arbiters of broadcasting in the Federal Republic fail to appreciate the implications of the decisions that will face them in the near future, if they act out of political self-interest or with an eye only for misguided economies of the short term, they will, with their decisions, mould a turning-point in the history of West German broadcasting and of West German society on which future generations will look back with anger and sadness. The moment of crisis is the moment of greatest opportunity.

CHAPTER FIVE

Towards a Closer Definition of Public Broadcasting

Since 1961 when the Federal Constitutional Court gave broad-casting in West Germany its classical legal foundations, there has been a considerable change in the political and economic climate, and life in West Germany has settled at last to something that would elsewhere count as normalcy; the need has therefore arisen to extend and complement the basic definitions of 1961 – par-ticularly at points either obscured at the time by the predominant issue of public or state control, or given only superficial thought by the *Länder* in the buoyant mood of victory. In the late 1960s and early 1970s two sets of relationships which affect broadcasting have emerged as problems and are progressing only slowly to-wards a solution as the broadcasting system approaches the potential turning-point into the age of its maturity. Crucial to the debate is still the quintessential definition of the meaning and seat of public control in broadcasting. A closer definition of this has been made necessary, on the one hand, because of the efforts of the political parties to influence broadcasting and because of the resultant reactions of the broadcasters themselves – a complex set of relationships between the public, the public's representatives, political representatives and broadcasters which is explored in detail in the second part of the book. On the other hand, the subject of this chapter, the relationship of public broadcasting with the commercial world and the world of public administra-tion, particularly the fiscal authorities, has been subjected to careful scrutiny. All these questions of conflict, differentiation and definition are aspects of the complicated process of determining the exact contours of the social and societal status of broadcasting.

The focal point in the process of reassessment is again a ruling of the Constitutional Court, significantly almost exactly a decade removed from the first: 27 July 1971.[1] This ruling is, in fact, one of a series of five which can be associated together in a mutually complementary pattern. At the time of writing two definitive rulings are still outstanding: the ZDF taxation case before the Federal Finance Court (Munich) and the technical ruling on the Saarland broadcasting law requested of the Federal Constitutional Court by the Saarland Administrative Court on 25 April 1974[2] in the *Freie Rundfunk AG* case.[3] The outcome of this latter case is quite predictable (apart from the technicality) – the private company does not have a right to broadcast simply because the possibility exists in the law. The ruling will, probably, fully complement that of the Federal Administrative Court (Berlin) of 10 December 1971[4] which finally set the seal on the fate of the *Fernsehgesellschaft Berliner Tageszeitungen mbH* (founded 1960).[5] The fifth case and the first in the series is the 1968 Post Office ruling.[6]

The courts have constantly upheld the monopoly position of public broadcasting and in so doing have provided some hints about when and how private, commercial interests might become involved. The main emphasis of the courts' thinking has been on the prevention of the control of broadcasting media by one individual or group. There seem to be two ways in which this difficulty could be overcome: one is technically still not possible – by giving every interested party the means to broadcast, so that a situation is created similar to that in the press; the other is feasible but difficult to implement – to ensure public control irrespective of the economic base of the enterprise. The principles involved in this latter possibility have implications also for the existing stations. The Federal Administrative Court (December 1971) was sceptical about the independence of any broadcasting body that is dependent on commercials for its income, a problem that is extreme in the case of commercial enterprise broadcasting where public participation and control would need the most meticulous guarantees, but which is incipient also in the existing stations – at least in some areas; some stations are financially dependent on income from commercial sources, in particular ZDF, which depends for almost 50 per cent of its income on advertising revenue. Commercial entrepreneurs interested in entering broadcasting have thus been set the target as a prerequisite for their involvement in devising a method of maintaining a balance between the commercial base and the public superstructure. The margins explored a little earlier in the ruling of July 1971, when the judges voted four to three in favour of the broadcasting authorities who had resisted the imposition of turnover tax (VAT) on their licence income, were at least as tantalizingly critical. Here the boundaries between commercial activity and public administration are seen to interfuse to the point where the dividing-line is almost untraceable. If and when the prime ministers of the *Länder* re-examine the system in its entirety, they would do well to heed this fact and strive to enhance the standing of broadcasting by distinguishing it clearly from all other activities.

The already blurred areas between the worlds of broadcasting, public administration and commercial enterprise had been made open interfaces by the practical consequences of the 1968 Post Office ruling, making the task of the judges in 1971 all the more difficult. In retrospect the former case was less remarkable for the wisdom of the ruling than for the then unforeseeable ramifications of it. The reactions of the Post Office were predictable: deprived of its accustomed predetermined portion of each and every licence fee, it began to set its charges according to its costs, greatly increasing the financial burden on the stations, with the result that they are now striving to make economies in their use of Post Office services and establishing their own licence collection centre in Cologne (due to open on 1 January 1976). If the Post Office aggravated the financial problems of the broadcasting authorities by its action, the *Länder* can be held guilty of making them impossible; they confused and misunderstood the role of the public broadcasting service – and also, at least in part, added a new and valid dimension to its significance. The *Länder* made the first of what may prove to be a series of regular licence increases to match increasing costs, coupling this with a demand for greater co-operation and rationalization in the system, with the establishment of wide-ranging criteria for licence exemption and with the standardization across the Federal Republic of all associated administrative regulations. They moved a small way towards a unified system by linking fees to costs, and they compensated by emphasizing the social aspect of the service.

If one ignores the fact that the exemptions were made at the expense of the broadcasting authorities, who suffered cuts in their potential income almost large enough to offset any gains from the increase in licence fees,[7] the fact remains that the *Länder* transferred to the broadcasting authorities the performance of a social service which should clearly be the responsibility of the public administration. They have also, in their nationwide rules and their demands for co-operation, related broadcasting more to the general public of the Federal Republic than to the various publics of the individual *Länder*. And in the relation of licence fees to costs, coupled with the demands for rationalization and economies, they have placed the system on a footing close to that of commercial enterprise. While it is true that a public broadcasting service should be available to all, that it should not squander its funds and that it should be given (or acquire) enough income to cover its costs, the problem in the Federal Republic now is that these elements have not been properly synthesized; the broadcasting authorities fall between three stools – they can be treated as a substitute for the welfare state, as commercial enterprises, or as public corporations (with at least a toe in the commercial world).

In this situation it is very difficult to define clearly the relationship of public broadcasting to the public, the public authorities and the business world. One anomaly that is apparent in the ZDF taxation case and was the subject of the Constitutional Court's attention in 1971 lies in the subjection of a public service, which has clear social obligations and an unquestioned significance for the whole of society, to taxation at the hand of the public authorities because its business management betrays commercial features. The web is, indeed, tangled; and the ruling of 1971 did not in itself resolve the problem. The importance of this ruling lies in the arguments of both the majority and the minority judges; together they contain analyses of all points relevant to the securing of the broadcasting system against illicit influences – including the fiscal authorities whose demands would undermine the freedom of public broadcasting as surely as would political or commercial infiltration.

Both opinions endorsed the principles established in 1961 and, because one group upheld the arguments of the broadcasting authorities and the other supported the position of the fiscal authorities, together they cover all points of relevance to the classification of licence dues in the spectrum of sources of income and of relevance to the definition of the status of the broadcasting service in a pluralistic society. Although the split decision tends to suggest incompatibility, the two analyses are in many ways complementary; it is far from difficult to build up a composite picture in which the role and status of public broadcasting are thrown into sharp relief.

The dissenting judges viewed licence income in relation to the production costs of broadcasting and referred to the 1970 increase to support this interpretation; they described licence income as a payment for the programme received and for the facilities needed for transmission. The vehicles for radio and television programmes, as seen by the three, appear as giant production and service undertakings that are no different from any others in the public sector and as such fully susceptible to taxation on their turnover.

The opposite view, taken by the broadcasting authorities and supported by the majority vote, argued that licence fees constituted a fund for the presentation of programmes irrespective of whether these programmes are received or not; no exchange as such is made so that there is no payment for a specific reciprocal service. Here broadcasting is seen as an aspect of public administration undertaken on behalf of the state, which is itself disqualified as the agent. As a corollary the four judges saw the activities of the broadcasting authorities as different from transactions in keeping with the private sector of commerce for which the tax in question is essentially reserved.

The four drew a distinction, as it were, at the top of the commercial sector – including broadcasting in the public (state) administration bracket. Their three colleagues drew the line at the bottom of the state sector and lumped together the public and commercial enterprise areas. The distinction they make is convincing, at least from one point of view: it rests on the difference between

> purely sovereign ('social') action by public institutions and activity of an 'authoritarian' nature which is characterized by the use, founded in and limited by the law, of the medium of state power which allows the use of force.[8]

One argument assesses broadcasting from the business point of view, making a classification dependent on where funds are actually used; the other sees the production side of broadcasting merely as a means to an end, the all-important programme through which broadcasting fulfils its 'integrative function in the totality of the state'.[9] Neither view admits a possible third area in which they would complement each other and in which also any inherent contradictions would disappear: broadcasting exists at a point between the various sectors of state, public administration and commercial enterprise, its social and societal significance places it beyond the reach of the fiscal authorities and because the final product, the programme, is all that is important, it is permitted to set its income (from whatever source) at a level necessary to guarantee a final product of the requisite quality, the existing control structures would allow adequate supervision.

The judges did not seek to establish these guarantees of broadcasting freedom, but they did discuss the priorities of public broadcasting – extending the lines of argument of 1961 to make them significant in the 1970s. Again their views are different and complementary; again, by relating the two, broadcasting can be placed in the framework of society with convincing nicety.

The majority judges described broadcasting as 'a matter that concerns the general public',[10] emphasizing in this respect the role of the broadcasting council as an organ of control representing the public at large and making an essential correlation between it and the external structures of broadcasting, particularly those that promote co-operation across the Federal Republic and between the two channels in television. Because the *Land* authorities and the broadcasting authorities operate in this way, broadcasting can be treated as an integrated whole, a *Gesamtveranstaltung*. It would not be too difficult to contest this view with examples drawn from practice, but this would not invalidate it as an interpretation which takes broadcasting right out of the commercial sphere and also expresses succinctly the ideal the system must aim to realize in the 1970s: a broadcasting service designed and protected in its internal and external structures so that it can guarantee to meet the public need and serve the public interest. The old ideal of the direct link with the public is here allied with the new perspective of a nationwide service.

The dissenting judges went somewhat further in their analysis;

[71]

they defined in outstandingly relevant and unambiguous terms the protected area of public control. They stated clearly where the seat of democracy in broadcasting is, distinguishing it from the areas of state administration and also of broadcasting itself; their view allows a definition of a defensive barrier against state interference, against excessive influence by any one group, including politicians and broadcasting personnel, and against economic exploitation.

In this latter instance their position is, in fact, somewhat inconsistent: they want broadcasting protected from the influence of small groups with political and economic power and yet, indirectly, they would have weakened the position of the broadcasting authorities had they held the majority on the panel of judges – they would have penalized the stations because the *Länder* had strengthened them against the vagaries of economic trends. In the other areas their views are unexceptional.

Broadcasting cannot, by definition, be a function of the state, therefore the broadcasting authorities cannot act as agents for a form of state administration; rather, the judges argue, is the reverse the case: if the state assumes responsibilities in broadcasting it thereby takes upon itself a function of the public. Similarly unequivocal are their views on the division of labour in broadcasting: the *Länder* legislate to create a protective framework, the stations (whatever their legal form) provide the medium, and the public controls the form and content of the service provided; there are no nebulous interfaces.

The judges, without defining the public, make it clear that the concept of the groups relevant to society is still of fundamental importance. They were obviously influenced in their comments by events in broadcasting over the previous two years when the movement among programme personnel to establish and protect their own standing had caused many to think seriously about the meaning of democracy and control in broadcasting. The judges aimed their remarks ultimately at this group, but they are equally applicable to any strategically placed group which could exploit a privileged position at the expense of public control. The judges' view of control could be applied as a yardstick to the whole of the second part of this book. Control is exercised by the socially relevant groups acting through the relevant organs of the broadcasting houses and by the public at large, by individuals and groups who make their opinions known through their choice of programmes and by any other legal means available to them.

It follows from all this that the vehicles responsible for the fulfilment of the public task are not really 'masters' of radio and television and that even less may those professionally active in these vehicles see themselves as masters of radio and television, but that the vehicles are merely instruments by means of which the socially relevant forces and groups fulfil the public task.[11]

It is significant that all seven judges saw fit to discuss basic principles again in a ruling concerned ostensibly with taxation. Clearly they considered other issues to be of more fundamental importance, possibly because they felt they were endangered. It is indisputable that the financial problems of broadcasting, its taxation status and the source of its income are at present less of a threat to the public, democratic control of broadcasting than other forces which stand within and on the fringe of broadcasting. The broadcasters themselves are not free of blame in this respect, but the threat they constitute pales into insignificance beside the party-political invasion of public broadcasting.

The judges in the various courts have made comments that will enable the prime ministers to protect the broadcasting services from the public authorities and from commercial enterprise, to put the stations' commercial income (perhaps even the commercial programme) and their payments to the Federal Post Office into proper perspective; they have, above all, offered at a key moment in postwar broadcasting history a contribution to the understanding and definition of public broadcasting which could serve to remind those in authority in the *Länder* and in the broadcasting stations of principles which must be observed as a basis for a solution to any problem, whatever its origin, in broadcasting. In theory, a position for public broadcasting outside any currently existing administrative and business category could be established with ease; in practice, it would serve no purpose if it were not accompanied by the honest transfer of the broadcasting service into the full control of its rightful masters, the public at large.

Part Two

Part Two

CHAPTER SIX

A Question of Balance

In the first part of the book the development of the present broadcasting system in the Federal Republic has been discussed in some detail. What has emerged since the war could be described as a working compromise of many varied, often divergent and sometimes conflicting elements. A large number of fully autonomous broadcasting houses have, through experience, arrived at a formula which allows them to continue to exist as independent bodies, protected from the central government and largely from the regional governments also, at a point in the political, economic and social system which, had it been defined in the abstract, must appear as no man's land. They continue successfully to exist by virtue of the balance that has been created between the federal government, the *Land* governments and society; they have safeguarded their existence by devising their own working division of labour and finding a complement to this, somewhat uneasily, in the mildly specialized programming of the three television channels. The financial foundations of the system are characterized by a compromise struck between the need for an essentially neutral source of income and the need to secure sufficient income to be able to continue to provide a full service to which the whole of society can have access: licence income is supplemented by income from commercial activities. With the commercial world at large a compromise has been reached which, as yet, has yielded up none of the fundamental independence of broadcasting.

In two areas a viable balance has yet to emerge: in the arrangements with the Federal Post Office and in the rather more difficult altercation with the taxation authorities. In both these questions a compromise solution will no doubt be reached. In the former case a solution is already mapped out in the development by the ARD of its own system for collecting licence fees; in the latter the outcome is far less clear, but as the attention of politicians and public focuses on it, a generally acceptable solution becomes more of a probability. Thus the system will continue to function, as it has in the past, because somehow a compromise will be created which properly embodies something of the spirit of the federal system.

It follows from all this that the system will be endangered if the balance is disturbed. If the balance is questioned even at one point, adjustment may become necessary at many other points; if it is destroyed – by accident or by design – even in one small area, the functioning of the whole may be impaired. If the balance in a key area of co-operation is lost, then the whole system could collapse – possibly with disastrous consequences for elements in the structure of West German society only very indirectly connected with broadcasting.

In this second part of the book the essential concept of balance will be examined in the context of the functioning of the system and of the individual stations. Thus a set of related areas is approached where in the early 1970s a crisis developed and came to a head, which has as yet not been finally resolved and which is of paramount importance for the future of West German broadcasting. This is the struggle for balance in a set of vital relationships at the centres of control in the system and in the stations. In recent years the equilibrium in West German broadcasting has not looked particularly secure; it has been shaken by changes in relationships between the ARD and ZDF, within the ARD and, the most critical area, within the individual stations.

SOME THOUGHTS ON THE MEANING OF BALANCE

On 5 November 1971 an article appeared in *Die Zeit* under the title: 'Crisis in German television: democracy at an end?' in which Wolf Donner discussed the tension developing at the time because ZDF was beginning to enjoy some sort of status. He saw the ARD being forced to increase the control of its own programmes, reducing (perhaps) something of the autonomy of the contributors to the first channel and introducing similarity rather than contrast into the balance between ARD and ZDF. The same author took up the latter point in a longer article ('A row in the playground. Cultural programmes in television under attack') in the same edition of *Die Zeit* and analysed in detail the problem of the relationship between cultural and political programme content with particular reference to the impossibility of finally segregating the two without completely emasculating both:

> Everywhere in the television stations petty polarization is apparent: politics here, culture there; this detracts from both and tends to cut out the in-between area, the free space which is clearly so dangerous, where socio-cultural and, of course, also political analyses and predictions are made and thought stimulated.

The article ends with a hint at the root cause of this somewhat negative development:

> ... the formation of party-political fronts, the anxious tactical manœuvring in all directions, the increasing influence of political apportionment and the incipient election campaign all make for an even more sterile balance – before long in culture as well.

The emphasis in both articles is on a loss of flexibility; the give in the system was diminishing as those involved tried to take more for themselves. Polarization is anathema in a public system, particularly in the broadcasting media, and all the signs in the early 1970s – correctly read by Donner – indicated increasing polarization with an accompanying stultification of the system. Donner's main concern was the programme on the air, for it is here that the question of balance is at its most apparent. The hint regarding the tactical manœuvrings and the increase in party-political apportionment indicates, however, that the root cause lies deeper.

The stations, in the persons of the intendants, have been under attack for some time from two different quarters; they have been caught in a pincer movement by two opposed forces, the controlling groups and the production teams. The two main parts of the discussion below are concerned with the rise of party-political forces through the legally constructed channels (only rarely in open contravention of them) and, secondly, with the nature of the movement among programme personnel to secure certain safeguards against illicit influences. Both these developments present obvious dangers to the position of the intendant and it is he who

[79]

most directly embodies and upholds the balance of the system; if the position of even one intendant is undermined, so important is each in the system as a whole, then the repercussions can and will be felt throughout the system. The intendant has to be an artist of balance; the problems of the system can always be related to a greater or lesser extent to the role and status of the intendant.

However, the concept of balance is far from simple; to discuss it in detail and relate it to the responsibilities of the intendant would overstretch the framework of the present volume. From an exhaustive discussion of balance literally nothing relating to broadcasting could be omitted. For example, it would have to include:

> broadcasting freedom, the 'principles for programming' in the broadcasting laws, the supervision of broadcasting, proportionalism in staffing, elections of intendants, the television joint programme and the function of the third radio programmes; questions are posed about co-determination for broadcasters, about statements of fact in programmes and about the right of reply, about opinions and counter-opinions in the programmes, about the relationship of programme-makers to listeners and viewers, about the nature of licence fees and who determines their use, the training of broadcasting producers, the securing of a necessary measure of flexibility in the personnel structures of the stations, the equality of social security for journalists in broadcasting and in the press, the function of broadcasting in our society and also of the individual journalist and whether this is different in broadcasting and in the press, and if so, why? And so on, and so on. Almost the whole package of broadcasting and programme policies is under debate.[1]

In the final analysis broadcasting policy and programme policy cannot be definitively separated the one from the other; in so far as they can, however, it is the former that comes closer to the theme of the present work. In thus defining the field more closely, however, the difficulties of German terminology must not be forgotten; *Rundfunkpolitik*, in keeping with the all-too-many words formed with such ease and genuine idleness by tacking '-*politik*' (or, occasioning even more difficulty, '-*politisch*') on to an otherwise fairly accessible term, can be translated in a number of related but nonetheless different ways, of which two – 'broadcasting policy' and 'broadcasting politics' – merely hint at the spectrum of possible nuances of meaning. Without extending the translation exercise, it is useful to devote some scrutiny first of all to the second, less directly relevant concept, *Programmpolitik*, to throw into relief the problem of balance in this respect.

A comment on the translation of the term 'balance' is essential, because here some important elements of meaning are lost in English. The idea of balance can be expressed in German by a number of words; here the one used is *Ausgewogenheit*, which implies a quality of 'having been weighed out'. It is significantly different from the foreign loan word *Balance* so often used (loosely) by politicians, for which the correct German term – except in its subtlest undertones – might be *Gleichgewicht* ('equal in weight', 'in equilibrium'). A standard German dictionary[2] lists only the verb from which *Ausgewogenheit* derives: '*auswiegen: genau wiegen; im einzelnen wiegen*' – to weigh exactly, to weigh in individual units (literally: in detail). *Ausgewogenheit* has a narrower meaning than the English 'balance' and implies that detailed measurements are made. With this the root of the problem of balance in relation particularly, but not solely, to the programme is exposed; the word is used with optimistic looseness while, inevitably, it encourages 'weighing up and out'. Much of the uncertainty and many of the problems of the West German broadcasting system arise because the temptation to try to create a balance by counting minutes or heads has not yet been overcome.

A noteworthy observation is made by Herbert Janssen in the article quoted above:

> None of the existing broadcasting laws, inter-*Land* agreements and standing rules of the broadcasting houses contains explicit reference to balance in the programmes. What is referred to everywhere is the responsibility of the respective intendant for the programme.

The concept of balance exists only as a guiding principle which was formulated outside the sphere of broadcasting. It was, in fact, also formulated outside the sphere of politics and outside the sphere of the socially relevant groups; it was first enunciated by the guardian of the rights of all these groups, the Federal Constitutional Court, in 1961. The court recognized that the rights of all socially relevant groups to representation on the controlling bodies of the broadcasting stations must be complemented in the programme, which must reflect 'a minimum measure of balance in content, impartiality and mutual respect'.[3] The judges had in mind, it seems, some concept of fair play, but as so often happens one word has been emphasized out of context; most commonly and consistently here it is the element of flexibility, the idea of a (necessary) minimum that is lost.

Since 1961 the concept of balance has been discussed many times over, so that when the members of the second Michel Commission[4] offered their comments on it in 1970, they had the advantage of extra experience both of the practical issues involved and of the main points under debate. They proceeded from the idea of neutrality, thus revealing the turning taken by public broadcasting as a result of the preoccupation with balance. Neutrality of a kind is certainly implied when many shades of opinion have to be balanced in one medium, but there is no suggestion that there must be a complete expunction of opinion; the contrary, in fact, is intended:

> Neutrality, as a task set for broadcasting, (is) in no way identical with a kind of abstinence from things political or even party-political, nor with a limitation of broadcasting to the 'communication of value-free information'. Similarly neutrality in no way makes it obligatory to even out all contrasting opinion into a non-committal and innocuous, shallow ideology of the general weal, or to conform and think in terms of political apportionment. Differing opinions, incisive analyses, agreement with the individual views of a political group are permissible in individual programmes as long as the right of immediate reply for the other group, the right to present the other opinion is guaranteed, as long as broadcasting in its entirety is not attached to one political group and the balance of differing opinions and therefore also a general impartiality is guaranteed. Neutralization, therefore, does not mean a levelling-off of the selection offered, it means simply that the programmes are not pre-determined to the line of any given social or political power group.[5]

The commissioners thus went to great lengths to clarify the import of the concept of balance; they obviously thought this incumbent upon them and equally necessary because of abuses in the system which were threatening to rob it of much of its value, undermining its key function in the democratic state of facilitating the formation of informed and meaningful opinion.

SOME ASPECTS OF BALANCE IN PROGRAMME PRACTICE

Two developments in the late 1960s which the Michel commissioners deprecated were featureless mediocrity and overweening partisanship, particularly the latter. Both trends were products of the attitudes and activities of the major political parties, in particular possibly of the CDU which was for the first time out of office and thus somewhat out of the limelight.

The activities of the parties within the stations form the burden of a later chapter; here their reactions rather as members of the viewing and listening public will be illustrated.

The counting of minutes and seconds must certainly be recorded as one of the most extreme examples of the loss of balance which results from a preoccupation with balance. In early 1971, for example, *Der Spiegel* reported[6] that the CDU had enlisted the aid of the *Konrad-Adenauer-Stiftung* to observe the equality of opportunity accorded the parties in television news programmes; it was claimed that both ARD and ZDF reported four times as often about the SPD-FDP coalition as about the CDU/CSU, respectively government and opposition. A timed sample over seven weeks of HR broadcasts had already shown the SPD receiving 150 minutes of radio time and the CDU only 50, while the CDU had had 42 opportunities to be heard on television and the SPD over 100.

No matter how patently stupid, this sort of activity does exert pressure on the people who make the programme – to the extent, for example, where the editor-in-chief of the ARD news broadcasts (DFS) felt compelled to issue a statement correcting the false impression given by an article in *Die Welt* (15 November 1972). He refuted in detail the information contained in the article which had attempted to highlight apparent discrepancies in the treatment of the parties: 1,700 seconds for the SPD-FDP, 484 for the CDU/CSU. The correction included a different total for the two groups and suggested a different interpretation of the figures,[7] showing that the madness had spread into the stations, causing the broadcasters themselves to count seconds – hardly a situation conducive to free reporting.

The situation to which the NDR *Redaktionsausschuss* (committee

[83]

representing programme production staff) reacted in a letter to the chairman of the CDU parliamentary party in the *Bundestag*, Professor Carstens, was more serious.[8] The broadcasters supported their intendant, who had already refuted the accusation of a lack of balance in the early morning news commentaries, and then went on to censure severely the action of Jürgen Echternach, chairman of the CDU in Hamburg, who had, they said, taken unfair advantage of his position as chairman of the NDR administrative council to demand time in these early morning commentaries. The broadcasters comment: 'We fear that actions of this kind can serve only to intimidate those responsible for and who work on these programmes.'

Again this example is best assigned to the lunatic fringe; the impact of the early morning commentaries is probably not great, and overt attacks, although they seem to intimidate, do provoke an overt response (for example, the published letter); they probably also provoke a (less overt) response in other programmes. The general tendency is however apparent, and when large audiences are involved, as in the major television magazine programmes transmitted at peak viewing hours during the evening, the question becomes critical. Here the balance between ARD and ZDF and across the ARD first-channel programmes becomes important. Often the political colouring of a programme will depend on the station which produces it, the bias of the station itself reflecting the political climate in the area it serves. Because of this, perhaps inevitable, bias, some programmes begin to be unacceptable in areas with differing political convictions; a left-wing proclivity will not be particularly welcome in a predominantly CDU or CSU area. The two magazine programmes that are most often the centre of controversy are the ARD *Panorama*, broadcast from Hamburg, and the *ZDF-Magazin*; the latter because of its ultra-conservative approach[9] and the former because of its left-wing leaning. However, the balance within the ARD programme itself involves a more interesting set of relationships than that between ARD and ZDF. In the first channel *Panorama* (SPD) is complemented, for example, by *Monitor* (FDP) and *Report* (CDU/CSU), the latter two from Cologne and alternately Munich and Baden-Baden; the four stations offer productions in a balanced rotation at the same time each week, so that one view is not predominant at that programme time. The accusation of consistent bias in each (as indicated) is often made, but whether the claims can be fully substantiated and whether the individual biases balance each other out over the cycle is not particularly important here; the point at issue is how a programme, particularly one of this importance, which appears to subscribe fairly consistently to an identifiable party-line, can be reconciled with the principle of balance.

The intendants, whilst denying that there is a case to answer, have taken a narrow view.[10] Their opinion is that each broadcaster should be permitted to make his own impact on a programme, but that it is wrong for a whole programme always to bear the same stamp. A programme should not be readily identifiable with a given party, even if something of a balance is maintained by other similar programmes; over a reasonable period of time, each programme should be seen to represent a spectrum of opinion within itself. The problem for the ARD thus becomes apparent; the question of balance encroaches upon the sovereignty of the individual stations whose programmes could, under these rules, become progressively less differentiated.

Clashes have arisen within the ARD over unacceptable programmes. A few stations have used their right not to transmit a programme and have substituted something of their own; BR has taken this step most often, but so far the instances have been few and far between. The fact that the right to opt out is so little used is a remarkable achievement in a system of the complexity of the ARD; it is also a guide to the proper perspective of the problem of balance at this level. Nonetheless, the balance of the ARD programme has been the subject of much discussion and this latter illustrates where the weaknesses lie – in the misinterpretation of the concept and in the consequent threat to freedom and flexibility.

ARD GUIDELINES

In 1970 SWF intendant Helmut Hammerschmidt initiated a discussion among his fellow intendants on a set of principles that could be used to bring an extra degree of reliability to ARD programming. These principles would be a set of supra-station guidelines which would complement rather than supersede the guiding principles which, in some shape or form, each of the individual stations already had. The potential effect of the original Hammerschmidt proposals would have been a general levelling-off of the programmes; however, after some six months of discussion (November 1970–June 1971), a set of six 'Principles for Cooperation in the ARD Joint Programme, *"Deutsches Fernsehen"* ' was formulated; this was a much shorter document and one with a clearly different slant from Hammerschmidt's 'Draft Guidelines for Political Programming'.[11] The proposals passed through several stages before they reached their final form; a broad view of the first and final versions will show how far-reaching and restrictive are the implications of even the simplest suggestions of new controls.

Hammerschmidt introduced his paper with a preamble outlining the change that he perceived in ARD programmes: because political elements were becoming increasingly apparent in every kind of programme, guidelines were becoming necessary for the handling of political content in whatever framework it appeared. This apparent predominance of the political was accompanied, in Hammerschmidt's view, by increased criticism of the existing order, criticism with overwhelmingly negative traits. Hammerschmidt also believed that it was essential to affirm the existing order and that, in this context, it was inappropriate to see one type of programme as balancing another – pluralism must be promoted in each type of programme.

It is interesting to note that although Hammerschmidt's paper deals in part with the concept of balance, the term he uses is 'plurality' – a much more appropriate and positive concept.

The paper leaves no doubt that Hammerschmidt detested one thing above all others: the tendency of broadcasters to include their own opinions in virtually all programmes. This he saw as a result of the movement among broadcasters for more freedom – which was becoming increasingly the freedom to express a personal opinion when the journalist's real freedom had always been the freedom to report. Hammerschmidt does not plead for the exclusion of opinion, he asks for restraint – a vital part of the journalist's duty; opinion which is part of a situation is a necessary fact, the opinion of a reporter is not and it must be kept to a minimum and clearly identified for what it is.

Hammerschmidt's antidote to these tendencies forms the main (fourth) point of his paper: the restoration to its rightful place of the 'dialectical method' of presenting material. By this he means the inclusion of all relevant information in one programme: facts, arguments and opinion.

There are two particularly interesting points in the long discussion of techniques. One derives from the need to include all relevant material in one programme. Hammerschmidt hints that if one important body of opinion refuses to be represented, then it might become necessary to shelve a whole programme – hardly a move in the direction of balance. The second, rather strange idea is the concept of 'appropriateness' which he links with audience size: reporting a small item of local news in a national news programme would be inappropriate. It is difficult to see how the same criterion could be applied across the spectrum of an evening's viewing or listening.

Hammerschmidt reacted strongly to the implications as he saw them of the broacasters' movement for more freedom, to what might be loosely termed 'left-wing' trends in political and social journalism. On these points he is close to the views of the CDU/CSU; it is implied that any criticism of the existing order that is not positive can be classed as left-wing subversion and, worse, as bad journalism. There is also an implied move to protect the south German ('right-wing') stations from the influence of their north German ('left-wing') colleagues. There is in these parts of Hammerschmidt's document a dangerous tendency to argue for common ARD standards which would even out individual differences and reduce all contributions to the joint programme to the lowest common denominator agreed by all.

The intendants, rather than set up an exhaustive list of disqualifications, used the discussion of the proposals to search out a few universally valid principles, taking up the undoubted criteria of good journalism emphasized by Hammerschmidt. In their six principles they underline *inter alia* the need for balance and objectivity in the overall programme and in its component parts, for plurality and relevance – particularly in informational programmes; they want a clear separation of information from commentary, care in the presentation of facts and fairness in all the accompanying circumstances of interviews. Their principles of co-operation are a testimony to tried and trusted practice and constitute a flexible and constructive journalistic code.

The list of principles is preceded by an interesting preamble which provides an essential perspective. It establishes, in the first place, that the intendants do have the responsibility for the joint programme and then underlines the federal principle:

> Since the programme principles in the laws are in part formulated differently, differing interpretations of the substance and limits of broadcasting freedom cannot be excluded. Therefore the decision whether a programme will be transmitted in a given region must be left to the individual station.[12]

This precludes any lowest common denominator, but there is tacked on to it one final sentence which seems to have been forced in by the timid members of the conference, and has since proved the weakest part of the whole document: 'The stations will inform each other fully about any programmes which could be borderline cases in the terms of these principles.' The suggestion is vague enough to cause unlimited confusion and to open up the whole area of uncertainty that Hammerschmidt was attempting to remedy; it does not define the borderline case, who informs whom, who exactly is involved – the intendants only, or their deputies at various levels, or even the programme advisory bodies.

The vagueness of this arrangement, in a sense, typifies the attitude of the intendants as a body. In setting out their principles, they were careful to avoid any reference to controls and supervision; they left the system to work out its own solution. Hammerschmidt had not been so wise; the final paragraph of his paper reads:

> For this purpose (the implementation of guidelines – AW) it seems to me important to set up a guideline commission (which could be given a different name) which in future would deal with such cases in the joint programme as need further clarification. It would examine these cases, receive all the necessary materials for this and submit a report with a recommendation to the conference of intendants.[13]

The idea of central supervision over the implementation of the principles raises a point inherent in a situation in which an attempt is being made to create and maintain a balance between very disparate elements. There is the constant danger when the *Deutsches Fernsehen* is discussed that the easy mistake will be made of seeing the whole programme as the product of a single unit comparable with ZDF. Nor is this always an error made by the uninitiated;

various bodies of opinion involved in broadcasting – some in the ARD – have hinted at moves to unify it more, to give it an image with the same degree of identity as ZDF.[14] However, none of these suggestions has had a lasting impact, and the intendants' guidelines remain the sole instrument of control.

A recent incident provides an example of the way the ARD system works under the guidelines. The *Panorama* team intended to include in the programme for 11 March 1974 a contribution to the debate on the legalization of abortion in the form of information and discussion centred around one method of abortion and including parts of a film made during an actual abortion by this method. Almost at the last moment the intendants discussed the item and most of them, but not all for the same reason, were against broadcasting it. The programme was (an important point) not vetoed; the intendants do not have the right to veto a programme, they have the right to refuse it for their own area. This is effectively what they did, although the situation was somewhat complicated by the fact that only a part programme was involved. The new NDR intendant, Martin Neuffer, feeling that he might be the only intendant showing the film, decided to withdraw it in the interests of the system. The problem was resolved by agreement, control was by consensus and not by veto or proscription. The lesson imparted by the incident, ignoring the many interesting side-issues, was that the system set up in 1971 would work if a proper flow of full and timely information about impending programmes from the producing stations to the receiving stations could be ensured. Even as they dealt with this extremely delicate test case the intendants took pains to point out that no further extension of the guidelines was contemplated.[15] As a body they did not lose sight of the need to avoid cast-iron rules and standardized central procedures. They remained convinced that, to enable it to work, the system needed a minimum of control, a flexible balance.

THE PROBLEM OF IDENTITY

The position of the intendants in 1974 was still very much what it had been in 1971; they were concerned less with political attitudes and more with journalistic responsibility. The ultimate object of all discussion, whether on guiding principles or on individual programme content, was to preserve the joint programme without reducing it to a state of uniform mediocrity. The abortive *Panorama* attempt to swing opinion in an important public debate did, however, indicate that breakdown is a constant threat. In one sense the intendants face an impossible task; they have to create a balanced DFS and it has, at the same time, to be a programme that is acceptable and appropriate to 11 different *Länder*. The problem can be posed as a series of questions which highlight the major difficulties that have to be resolved. What exactly is the status and significance of a programme produced, say, by journalists in Hamburg and transmitted by DFS via SR to viewers in the Saarland? What are the implications for the viewers in the Saarland in terms of their balanced viewing? What are the implications, in terms of the joint programme transmitted over the whole of the Federal Republic, for the voice of the Saarland – should it, for example, have an opportunity to transmit via the ARD a programme of equal status to viewers in the NDR area?

The problem is one of identity. Each intendant has the right to balance the programme in his own area by opting out of the ARD programme and substituting material of his own choice. This does not happen often because the larger stations, which could afford to opt out, are well represented and do not need to, while the smaller stations, which are not well represented, cannot afford to opt out; the balance holds them together, as also does a belief in the system they have created. What the individual intendant cannot do is increase his agreed share in the joint programme – he cannot promote the image of his station, of the area it serves, at will outside that area. The limit to a station's right to project its image is set by its relative economic strength, itself a factor of relative population size. It could be argued that this basis for the composition of the DFS programme is not meaningful in terms of the whole of society.

The problem of identity has recently become a topic for discussion, mainly as a result of comments made by broadcasters and politicians in the SWF area; they see the balance as it is set for the system at present, coupled with the lack of restraint on the part of the larger contributors, as beginning to work against them. The SWF case, as put by both the intendant and his director of television, Dieter Stolte, in April 1974,[16] rests on the proportion of the West German population that resides in the SWF area (11 per cent), the portion of the ARD programme contributed by SWF

(8 per cent) and the additional financial commitment of SWF to the equalization fund (DM6.25m) – when most of the fund goes to support the smaller stations and DLF. Similar arguments were aired at about the same time in the Baden-Württemberg *Landtag* in response to a parliamentary question,[17] but here the motivation was more political, revolving around the problem of how far SWF and SDR viewers should be burdened with NDR *Panorama* programmes, how long these same people should be expected to contribute financially to maintain the highly favoured position of RB, SFB and SR, and why there was not more control of what was included in the ARD programme (with particular reference to political content). Although this argument in this forum is politically the more dangerous, the broadcasters' complementary argument is more meaningful in terms of public broadcasting. Stolte's main point is a strong one: 'It is extremely difficult for a station that has to contribute 8 per cent of the joint programme *Deutsches Fernsehen* to make itself recognizable in that joint programme.'[18] He admits that it is possible, when one television genre has been developed as a particular expertise, but when the station's efforts are spread over a wide area (including a once-in-four-weeks' magazine programme) it is not possible for its identity to emerge in the only place where it can exist – in the programme; the workers within the station and its public have nothing to identify with. He is raising a vital point about the psychology of broadcasting: the essential team spirit which is engendered by the public's reactions as well as by the efforts of production staff. Stolte made his point at a crucial moment in the development of West German broadcasting, when the constant demand is for economy and rationalization, when the stations are being forced into very narrow straits. His comment goes to the heart of ARD federalism which depends on a proper mix of individual identities, of different values without the loss of individual characteristics in some grey, homogeneous whole.

There is clearly a danger in the present economic climate of some loss of individual identity; there is also a threat to the continued existence of some stations. The point is often raised, both directly and indirectly, about the value of maintaining the smaller stations, because they are a financial burden on the system. RB is most often attacked in this way, for it has no strategic importance in terms of international politics and it stands directly at the side

of the massive NDR; it offers a constant test of the fundamental
principles of broadcasting in the Federal Republic. The supporters of RB do not think in economic terms, nor do they think
in terms of a simply proportional balance across the system,
they are concerned about viable federalism; all other arguments
are, by comparison, ultimately of selfish motivation and thus
imply a denial of the system.

The 'purist' argument is nowhere better put than in the comments of the one member of the Michel Commission who
completely dissociated himself from what his colleagues had said.
His words reveal a deep understanding of the *raison d'être* and of
the present problems of the West German system:

> The formula 'co-operative federalism' becomes unconvincing, it
> loses its motivation to solidarity, when the demand for stations (or
> *Bundesländer*) which are economically as self-sufficient as possible or
> even equally strong becomes the overriding principle. One is almost
> tempted to say: if there were no poor stations, then one would have
> to invent them, for the sake of co-operation and joint responsibility.
> It could become even more apparent in the next few years than it is
> now, that the real burden on the German broadcasting structure
> does not come from the small stations, but from the large ones
> which in terms of finance and capacity are so able to stand on their
> own feet that they see the obligations which derive from the ARD
> agreements as onerous tasks to be fulfilled only in so far as is
> absolutely necessary.[19]

The larger stations were certainly the major worry of the SWF
broadcasters and politicians and they are, as the discussion of
internal structures will show, a major problem in the system for
other reasons. However, whatever approach one takes to the
question of balance, if it involves proportional measurements it
can lead only to destructive dissension. The arbiters of the system
need a sure eye for what is right in terms of meaningful broadcasting and a good measure of charity to leaven their federal
principles.

THREE EQUAL CHANNELS?

Although the first programme is a composite creation and there is
not one but many third programmes, the public often sees the
television it is offered as three simple units. Something of this

error of perception is beginning to creep into the relations between the channels. Just as the ARD responded to the establishment of the ZDF image, so now (1974) ZDF is beginning to react to the incipient blossoming of the third channel. With a number of changes in the content of some of the third programmes, these have begun to offer a new degree of competition to the two major programmes. Professor Holzamer, ZDF intendant, has accused the ARD of developing a third full programme out of what was intended as a minority service.[20] At the root of his worries is the ubiquitous problem of insufficient funds, for he sees the third channel as consuming an unjustifiable measure of the total funds (25 per cent of ARD licence income and 18 per cent of the grand total) and in return stealing viewers, thus reducing the value of the second channel to the advertising world. There is in his remarks a strange suggestion that the ARD had used the programme co-ordination agreement to bind ZDF and then increased its own manœuvrability by extending the range of the third channel. The feeling of insecurity that prompted this thought reveals one of the inherent weaknesses in a system where all the stations – including ZDF – in all their programmes are servants of the same masters and yet are forced, because of the lack of real insight into the significance of this fact, to vie with each other in disintegrative competition.

Professor Holzamer suggested some modifications which he would welcome in the third programmes. He advocated a return to their original function of providing for educational, regional and minority needs; he suggested that they should repeat material from the other two channels where there is a demand for it and that they should carry the programmes for foreign workers. His ideas certainly warrant careful consideration; they aim to eliminate the sort of competition that could lead to three similar programmes, they try to make some necessary savings while extending the scope of the two major programmes, and they face objectively the need for constructive programming for the foreign workers, who do not present a homogeneous group across the Federal Republic but live in quite different communities in different areas – a task for the regional services.

ARD reaction to ZDF interference in the affairs of the individual stations was initially hostile, with Holzamer accused of trying to dictate programming to the third channel. Since then, however, the questions raised have become a subject for discussion both within the ARD and between it and ZDF. It is clear though that the system as a whole is at present in an uneasy state. Certain areas are showing a tendency to turn inwards, to consider themselves first. The balance in the system is not fully viable, causing uncertainty, a lack of confidence, suspicion and fear. There is a lack of clarity about where the system is going – and these developments do not have their roots ultimately within the stations themselves. Although enlightened discussion between the intendants can go some way towards easing the tensions between them, to solve their problems they will have to direct their efforts elsewhere.

Many of the problems can be related to the system's weak economic base, to the alienation caused by the upsurge of the programme-makers, to the disregard of party politicians for the rules of the game – and these in turn can all be related to the general political climate. A minor revolution in attitudes will have to occur before these problems can be solved; the political disorientation which is delaying the removal of the inadequate economic arrangements and has led the politicians to invade the stations' sovereignty, thereby inciting the broadcasters to their action, will have to work itself out before the system can return to a positive, productive balance. All the attempts to define and control, to impose rigid rules on broadcasting – the counting of seconds, the desire to change the style of programmes, the thrusting forward of some stations at the expense of others, the jealous suspicion between the channels – are reactions to the same situation, to the one basic problem of security and sovereignty in broadcasting. The balance has been disturbed at the centres of control within the stations and, more significantly, in the political institutions and structures that are supposed to guarantee the freedom and pluralism of that control. The political forces in the Federal Republic have lost sight of the role and importance of a free broadcasting system; by implication they have lost sight of the principles of democracy and pluralism. The unease in broadcasting generally is a sign that this departure is no small matter; already it is infecting areas where the public mind, and public opinion will be affected; the perspective of the whole West German system of society could be in the balance.

Control in the West German Broadcasting System

The essence of a public broadcasting system is that it is a service for the public, controlled by the public; the broadcasting media are, in effect, a loop of public communication, keeping the public informed and articulate. The loop is, of course, far from simple in practice. The link between the broadcasting body and the public via the two broadcasting media is direct and uncomplicated; the link between the public and the broadcasting body, the mechanism by which public control is maintained, is far from direct and can be complicated to the point where its public origins are obscured.

The broadcasting institution in a public system is an agent appointed by the public to perform the service of broadcasting. The whole public, however, cannot join in appointing and controlling its agent; supervisory agents are introduced to perform the immediate functions of appointment and control. Again, the appointment and supervision of the second agent can hardly be implemented efficiently by the whole public, and so the services of a further intermediary are called upon. A chain of representatives and agents is very quickly built up – each, in effect, adding to the distance between the public and its media and at the same time increasing the possibilities of misrepresentation. It is a thoroughly characteristic procedure in systems of representative government; the way it works in West Germany reveals something of the quality of representative democracy in that country.

THE CONTROL STRUCTURES

In the Federal Republic the series of delegations by which public control of broadcasting is effected is virtually everywhere the same. The various acts of legislation governing the constitution of the broadcasting houses are superficially very similar, though detailed examinations reveal considerable differences in emphasis, inaccuracies, inconsistences and even unconstitutionalities. These differences and their consequences are sometimes significant enough to suggest the need for a full analysis of all existing legislation, including the accompanying standing rules. A perambulation through the minutiae of West German broadcasting legislation would, however, take the discussion far beyond the scope of the present volume; here the object is to uncover the chain of command from the public to the broadcasting institutions in its main variations and to discuss something of their relative strength or weakness.

All the stations but two (SFB, RIAS) have three main organs of control: the broadcasting council (*Rundfunkrat*), the administrative council (*Verwaltungsrat*) and the intendant. The balance of power between these three and their link with the public are the points where the differences between the two main models emerge. It would be enlightening, before embarking on a more detailed discussion of the functions and interrelationships of the three, to record the defining commentary of a body of experts on a configuration generally accepted as optimal. A number of relevant sources are available, of which the most useful is the report of the second Michel Commission, which contains a long and thorough analysis of the situation of broadcasting in the Federal Republic. Section G of part seven of the report is an analysis and discussion of the 'pluralistic internal structures of broadcasting' (the model held to be the best) and includes sections on the three main organs.

The broadcasting council is put into perspective in the following way:

> The broadcasting council is generally ... understood as the representative of the public or community in the field of broadcasting. It is under obligation to speak out for the overall interests of broadcasting and of its audience ...
> In the system of the different organs in a structure as complex as

that of the public broadcasting corporations, the functions of the broadcasting council can be compared with those of the legislature in the organization of the state. Incumbent upon it is the whole supervision of the station ... Besides its competence for general supervision, the broadcasting council has also a competence to supervise the intendant in respect of the programme ...

This competence to advise and supervise in respect of the programme ... is the responsibility solely of the broadcasting council.[1]

The administrative council is somewhat more easily defined:

Unlike the broadcasting council, the administrative council fulfils no representative functions, its activities are purely administrative. Accordingly its field of duties is to be demarcated from that of the broadcasting council ...

Its main duty lies in the supervision of the administrative functioning of broadcasting ... in supervising the intendant's management ... Consequently the intendant is responsible to it solely in questions related to business and administrative management.[2]

In their comments on the intendant, the members of the commission were obviously influenced by their awareness of the problems currently facing West German broadcasting:

In contrast to the broadcasting and administrative councils, the collegial organs of a broadcasting station, the intendant is a monocratic executive organ. In the field of broadcasting a collegial executive organ, a sort of collective leadership, would not only effectively neutralize and paralyse areas of responsibility, it would also, because of the inevitable party-political apportionment, lead to personal frictions which would inhibit its functioning. There are in the shape of the broadcasting council ... and administrative council ... sufficient organs of control available to counterbalance and prevent any excessive build-up of power by the intendant ...

The democratic legitimation of the intendant as a monocratic executive organ is guaranteed in his responsibility to the broadcasting council, which for its part represents the society in which broadcasting is founded.[3]

The interrelationship of the three organs is thus clear. It is the broadcasting council which embodies the public interest, as it is the focal point of the system; arranging and safeguarding the composition of this organ so that it always represents the public interest in the key position in the system is the crucial decision in any piece of broadcasting legislation.

The classification of the systems of internal control into two main categories is arrived at by an examination of the way the broadcasting council is constituted. The two basic models are the 'pluralistic' or 'social groups' model and the 'parliamentary' model. The former is the one found in the majority of the stations. The basic difference of principle, put simply, is that the *Landtag* ultimately determines the membership of the broadcasting council in the parliamentary model, whereas in the pluralistic model the groups relevant in society at large, which determine the character and quality of society, have the final say.

To establish details of the differences between the two models it is convenient to examine a few examples of broadcasting laws.

A COMPARISON OF CONSTITUTIONS

The HR law[4] is a generally accessible document which offers a useful basis for a series of comparisons. The legal platform for broadcasting in Hessen is a *Land* law which exemplifies the single *Land*, pluralistic model; it can be compared with a similarly pluralistic model where the broadcasting station serves more than one *Land*, where the act of constitution was an inter-*Land* agreement (SWF). A twofold comparison is then possible with a single *Land*, parliamentary model (WDR) and the inter-*Land*, parliamentary NDR.

The HR law falls into six sections with 22 paragraphs; the accompanying supplementary standing rules have five sections with 22 paragraphs.

Section one of the law (§1) sets out the legal form of HR as a corporation under public law, which has the 'right of self-administration and is not subject to state supervision'. Section two (§§2, 3) defines the station's task and the principles to be observed in the performance of it. Section three (§§4–16) outlines the rules for the internal organization of the station, including paragraphs on the broadcasting council (5–10), the administrative council (11–15) and the intendant (16). The remaining sections are devoted to licences (four), budgetary matters (five) and interim regulations which applied when the station was first founded in 1948 (first version only).

The importance of the standing rules varies from station to station; in HR they are simply a set of standing orders about the convening of meetings and the conduct of them, the payment of expenses to members of the supervisory bodies and methods of publicizing the business of these bodies. In some cases the law simply founds the station and the standing rules, which then take on the character of statutes, settle the details (e.g. SFB). The various standing rules will be left out of the discussion unless reference to them is essential to establish points not apparent from the respective law.

The work of the HR organs is covered by the general principles set out in section two, §3 of the law. These are approximately the same for all stations, the important points being:

1. Broadcasting is the business of the general public. It is carried out in complete independence impartially and it is to be kept free of every pressure to influence it.
2. Programmes are to provide ... (news, etc – AW) and to serve peace, freedom and international understanding.
3. Programmes may not offend against the constitution or the laws, nor offend moral and religious sentiments. Programmes are not permitted which contain prejudices or disparagements because of nationality, race, colour, religion, or the philosophy of life of an individual or of a group.
4. Reporting must be truthful and objective. . .

Independence and impartiality are clearly the two criteria which must be applied constantly to all aspects of broadcasting in the Federal Republic. The guarantees of independence and impartiality are the arrangements in the laws for the composition and functioning of the supervisory bodies, and in particular of the broadcasting council.

§5 (1) The broadcasting council represents the general public in the field of broadcasting. Its members are not representatives of a party, a confession, a professional or social class, or of an organization; they are not bound by instructions and may not be under contract to *Hessischer Rundfunk*.

(2) Each of the following sends one representative to the broadcasting council.

There then follows a list which commences with the *Land* government, the universities and the three major religious confessions, includes representatives of educational circles, of employees' and business interests, and finally ends with 'five *Landtag* deputies who are elected by the *Landtag* according to the principles of proportional representation'. The election of representatives is governed by (3) and (4), whilst (5) requires the number of women to be brought up to three, if the 16 seats listed have not yet yielded three or more women. The supernumerary women are to be drawn from 'working women who represent women involved in education and young people'. The *Land* government has the power to modify these rules.

The full period of office of the members of the broadcasting council is six years, with one-third of the members leaving office every two years in rotation; re-election is permitted. The political representatives change with changes in legislature and executive. If membership is terminated prematurely, a replacement completes the unexpired period of office. Suspension from office is effected by a vote of two-thirds of the broadcasting council (§6).

The main tasks of the HR broadcasting council are set out in §9; the first two are the most important:

1. To nominate and recall the intendant and to confirm the deputy appointed by the intendant.
2. To advise the intendant in fundamental questions related to the shaping of the programme and to see that the principles set out in §3 are observed.

The validification of the broadcasting council to fulfil its appointed tasks depends fundamentally on the rightness of §5(1) and (2) of the law. It is difficult to see how a representative under §5(2) is not a representative under §5(1) of the group or organization he is selected by. The representatives are chosen from a carefully balanced set of socially relevant groups so that a wide range of public tastes and interests will be taken into account. At the same time the overriding concern of the broadcasting council must be the quality of the broadcasting service; the members can hardly represent properly the interests of public broadcasting if they forget the interests of their base groups. What is interesting here is, however, not the semantic quibble, but whether the situation they operate in is conducive to their combining their dual roles; they are aided where the body they form is of moderate size and is composed of interests that range widely and do not fall into two or three obvious alliances. Once rigid divisions occur, members become no more than party votes. Only the political representatives in the HR broadcasting council are likely to divide into two opposing camps, and their number is strictly limited. It is instructive to examine briefly the HR broadcasting council from the two points of view of size and composition.

Sixteen, or at most 19, is a small enough membership for meaningful discussion and decision-making to take place; the number of interests represented is wide. The selection of members is carefully balanced to include all major opinion groups and also a number of members who could be expected to have quite relevant expertise. The basic rule of one representative per group is broken in the case of the *Landtag* representatives, possibly in the belief that these have an extra qualification as representatives of the public.

It could be argued that the extra representation of political groups is potentially a weakening factor in the work of the broadcasting council. These political representatives are, because they are elected in proportion to the strength of the parties, representatives of those parties and not of the *Landtag* as such. An additional factor of importance is the possibility that other groups will also delegate representatives who may be leading members of the political parties. In 1973 there were altogether eight *Landtag* deputies in a council of 19; in 1974, seven out of 19. Even if these seven or eight are divided, a group of four with a common policy is a strong, although not a decisive influence in a group of 19. Another section, less likely to be solidly united, could prove influential in the council: if the supernumerary women are counted, the educationist group could number eight – again not a majority.

The opposite end of the spectrum seems, on paper, to be the representation granted to the religious groups and particularly the economic groups; these latter seem disadvantaged with one representative each, who would generally be held, by their very nature, to be mutual opponents.

However, as the HR broadcasting council stands, it is not possible to find a convincing common denominator in terms of interest that would lead one to seriously suspect that its work could be determined by a recognizable group. The intention of the lawgivers to design an instrument for the pluralistic representation of the public is clearly apparent in the law and is borne out in practice.

On the nature of the membership of the broadcasting council, one further comment seems justified: it is most improbable that the members will be drawn from different social strata. They will all be leaders in their particular areas of activity, and this presupposes a certain level of education and, possibly, of income. Although one would not necessarily be justified in using the term 'elite' of them, they will belong to the establishment. At worst this means that their activities in broadcasting can only in the long term be in the interests of the establishment; at best it facilitates dialogue between them. What must not be forgotten in this context is that a supervisory body is under discussion and not the body of programme-makers; in the final analysis what matters is the understanding of the former for the work of the latter. The work of the station will be enhanced by a broadcasting council which is capable of constructive and open-minded discussion; it will be jeopardized by supervision that is no more than an attempt to implement rigid sectional policies. The composition of the HR broadcasting council would lead one to expect the former.

Of the paragraphs of the law that govern the composition and functions of the administrative council, §11(1), which sets out the membership, is all that need concern us here:

The administrative council is composed of:
1. The president of the *Landeszentralbank* for Hessen (*Land* central bank).
2. The president of the *Oberlandesgericht*, Frankfurt-am-Main (regional court of appeal).
3. A representative of the Technological University, Darmstadt.
4. Four members elected by the broadcasting council, who may not be under contract to *Hessischer Rundfunk* and may not belong to the broadcasting council.

In addition there have been, since May 1970, two members in an advisory capacity representing the HR personnel council.[5]

The HR administrative council has no direct political representation on it; it has three experts (two of them *ex officio*) from relevant areas (finance, law, technology), four representatives of the public interest, and two representatives of the broadcasting staff. The four members elected by the broadcasting council mark the point at which public control could become submerged by other, sectional interests; in HR the chances of this happening are not great. The balance of the organ is again neat and functional. In 1973–74 the members elected by the broadcasting council were all men with professional experience relevant to the management of broadcasting. The seven included one member of the *Landtag* only, the Hessen Minister of Finance – perhaps an obvious choice given the financial problems facing the broadcasting authorities.

In HR, as in all other stations, the administrative council concludes the contract with the intendant and represents the station in any differences at law with him. It has no say in the selection of the intendant, so that what could be a political decision taken by a small body is a matter entirely for the body representing the public. In many stations the administrative council has a hand in the choice of the intendant, either selecting him in consultation with the broadcasting council or selecting him for approval by the latter.

The unfussy style of the HR law is, perhaps, most apparent in the paragraphs that define the status and duties of the intendant. The first four clauses of §16 contain the information of relevance in the present context:

(1) The intendant is elected by the broadcasting council by a simple majority for from five to nine years. Re-election is permitted.
(2) The intendant represents the station in court and out of court. He requires the approval of the administrative council
(a) for the employment and dismissal of the business director (manager) and of the technical director,
(b) for other legal acts for which the standing rules require administrative council approval (mainly the purchase of property and investment – AW).
(3) The intendant directs and administers *Hessischer Rundfunk*. He arranges the programme in accordance with the laws.
(4) The intendant participates in the meetings of the broadcasting council, except when matters relating to him personally are to be dealt with; he has no vote.

In relation to (4), it must be remembered that the broadcasting council cannot issue instructions to the intendant, it can only advise him; on the other hand, it is obviously useful for him to hear its discussions. The attendance of the intendant at meetings of the administrative council is by request of either party.

In brief, the HR law is a commonsense piece of legislation which provides an uncluttered framework for the organization of the public broadcasting services in one *Land*. The body representing the public is not dominated by any one group, and the danger of this happening is small; it is certainly not dominated by the state. This body elects the intendant. The administrative council represents a balance of relevant expertise; its area of competence is clearly delimited and is different from those of the other two organs; it is not susceptible to the influence of one-sided vested interests. The intendant is faced with a necessary minimum of regulations. He is the watershed between the programme and the supervision, just as the broadcasting council marks the point where the contact between the state and the broadcasting authorities stops. The HR law is a model for the pluralistic control of broadcasting.

SWF was constituted by an inter-*Land* agreement[6] which, apart from the complications that arise out of these circumstances, reveals two differences in emphasis from the HR law: the separation of the sphere of public broadcasting from that of political government is less strict and the demarcation of competence between the two supervisory bodies is less precise.

§1 of the agreement gives the station the right of self-administration but does not exclude state supervision; the latter is, in fact, established explicitly in §19:

> It is the task of the *Land* governments (which act in rotation – AW) to watch over the orderly implementation of the regulations contained in this agreement and over the observation of the general stipulations of the law by the *Südwestfunk*.

The difference in attitude on this point of state supervision prompts an interesting question: how far is it constitutional for a government to set up a (public) body and not retain some modicum of supervision? Although the HR situation might seem ideal, one wonders whether a small area of final supervision which in no way infringes the freedom of broadcasting is not an extra guarantee of the proper functioning of the system. The fact that the government retains even a small right of supervision does, on the other hand, open up the way for the discussion of broadcasting matters, including programming, in the political organs of state – as, for example, happened in Baden-Württemberg in February 1974.[7] It is a very serious matter when the machinery of parliaments can be used to discuss questions that are properly the province of the body appointed by the public for this express purpose; an instance of this kind argues for the HR position, where the *Landtag* would in any case have enough legal grounds for action in a serious breach of the broadcasting code without its having to invoke the broadcasting law itself.

The different relationship between the three SWF organs and those of HR becomes apparent in the following clauses in the agreement:

§14 (1) The intendant directs the *Südwestfunk* according to the terms of the inter-*Land* agreement and of the standing rules. He is bound by resolutions of the administrative council.

§15 The intendant is elected for a period of four years by the broadcasting council and the administrative council in a joint meeting by a simple majority.

The standing rules mirror this overlapping of powers:

Article 12 (2): The chairman of the administrative council is to be invited to the meetings of the broadcasting council. Members of the administrative council have the right to attend meetings of the broadcasting council and to be heard. The intendant and his properly appointed deputy have the same right.

Article 14 (3): The broadcasting council and the administrative council can form combined committees from both bodies by concurring resolutions.

Article 32 (1): The intendant designates one of the directors or the legal adviser as his deputy with the approval of the broadcasting council and of the administrative council.

And all the senior appointments, the people the intendant can draw his deputy from, are subject to close control by one or other of the two councils:

Article 29 (2): The programme director is elected by the broadcasting council on the suggestion of the intendant ... He will not be elected and appointed for a period extending beyond the period of office of the intendant.

Article 29 (3): The technical director, the administrative director and the legal adviser are appointed by the administrative council in consultation with the intendant.

The division of powers in SWF is thus less clear than in HR; there is an opening left for state intervention and there is a close interrelating, in limited areas even a fusion, of the functions of the two councils; the freedom of the intendant is hedged in somewhat by the powers of the councils, particularly through their role in appointing senior staff – a power that could be used to influence programme policy.

The SWF structures show a shift in emphasis away from the broadcasting council towards the administrative council. This could denote a weakening of the link with the public; it could also be a means to improved efficiency and more positive supervision. The shift of emphasis becomes critical only if one reads the administrative council's power to issue directives to the intendant as including programming. It is possible that this arrangement helps to keep the larger, more cumbersome broadcasting council (49 members) in touch with affairs, and the smaller, more directly responsible administrative council (nine members) constantly aware of the public requirement.

The administrative council has three representatives of the *Land* governments (Baden-Württemberg two, Rhineland-Palatinate one) and six members elected by the broadcasting council. There are two advisory members who represent SWF personnel.[8] As with HR, the members cannot be members of the broadcasting council or of SWF; there are no rules about the number of political representatives, but the 6:3 proportion can be interpreted as representing the intended balance.

The composition of the broadcasting council, with the exception of two advisory members drawn from SWF staff, is arrived at by applying a formula set out in the agreement in tabular form (§10(2), §11(1): see Table 2). The members allocated originally to

Table 2. Formula for the composition of the broadcasting council

	Rhineland-Palatinate	Baden	Württemberg-Hohenzollern
Governments	1	1	1
Parliaments	4	2	2
Churches	4	1	1
Universities	1	1	1
Education	2	1	1
Youth organizations	2	1	1
Sports organizations	1	1	1
Trade unions	2	1	1
Chambers of commerce	3	1	1
Press	2	1	1
Municipalities and associations of municipalities	3	1	1
	25	12	12

Baden and Württemberg-Hohenzollern now accrue to Baden-Württemberg. The table is followed by a detailed breakdown of the groups whose representatives make up these numbers.

As with HR no rule exists to prevent the societal groups choosing active politicians as their representatives, but again an analysis of the broadcasting council yields no convincing evidence that it can be easily manipulated by any one body of opinion. Similarly it is unlikely that the administrative council, with the majority of its members elected by the broadcasting council, will be dominated by any one interest-group. There is some danger in the SWF arrangements that the interests of the public could be less well served than in HR simply because of the size of the broadcasting council and also, perhaps, because two large, distinct publics are represented. When the two councils meet together 58 members at least could be present, a rather large forum for efficient discussion and decision-making.

The importance of the size of the broadcasting council becomes apparent from an examination of the SWF standing rules which are quite complex; it is also reflected in the upgrading of the administrative council. The larger the broadcasting council, the greater the need for detailed regulations and the greater the degree of delegation to the less representative body. It seems not unlikely that a powerful administrative council and a comprehensive set of standing orders together constitute a strong factor of pressure on the broadcasters, not least on the intendant; the general effect could be rather inhibiting, perhaps even intimidating. It is, perhaps, not completely a coincidence that the discussion of guidelines for political programming in the ARD was initiated by the SWF intendant.

In spite of their differences, HR and SWF are both constituted according to a model which is designed to forge a strong link between the public and the broadcasters; the differences that arise are primarily a consequence of the relative size and uniformity of the geographical and political units the stations serve. SWF reveals some of the characteristics of a negotiated compromise.

The same differences in complexity apply to the two largest broadcasting stations in the Federal Republic – WDR and NDR, our examples of the parliamentary model; but the differences between this and our first, pluralistic model are of more fundamental importance than any characteristics of the individual statutes that reflect the nature of the area served.

A glance at the WDR law[9] will reveal an obvious new feature: the WDR organs number four, not three. The fourth organ is the *Programmbeirat*, which we shall translate as 'programme advisory committee' to make something of its status clear. It is an independent organ of the broadcasting body, but its role is purely advisory; it does not enjoy equal status with the other organs of control. The significance of the additional organ becomes clear when we recall that in both HR and SWF programming advice is the prerogative of the broadcasting council, which also chooses the intendant, who has ultimate responsibility for the programme; the supervision of the programme is the key area where public control must be as direct and effective as possible. The extra programme advisory committee can be seen as a device to separate with absolute clarity the areas of programming and administration; conversely it raises the question of whether programming is more effectively influenced and guided by an advisory committee or by a supervisory body with the power of appointment and dismissal.

An examination of the membership of the three WDR collegial organs will leave no doubt about the fundamental importance of the change in the control structures; the contrast with the HR model is complete.

Membership of the three organs is mutually exclusive and WDR staff are disqualified from membership. The members of the two councils are expected to have knowledge and expertise relevant to broadcasting and are required to be bound in no way by outside interests and directives (§8(5), §12(5)). Here the similarity with the other model ends; for example §8, clauses 1–3, read:

(1) The broadcasting council consists of 21 members.

(2) The *Landtag* elects the members of the broadcasting council and one deputy for each for a period of five years according to the principles of proportional representation. Re-election is permitted.

(3) Not more than four members and four deputies may belong to the *Landtag* or the *Bundestag*.

The principle governing the composition of the broadcasting council in the parliamentary model is thus revealed. The two other bodies emanate from the broadcasting council and therefore do not offer an inherent counterbalance to the influence of the legislature:

§9 (1): The broadcasting council elects the members of the administrative council and the members of the programme advisory committee named in §17 (2).

The administrative council has seven members, each elected for seven years, who leave office in rotation at the rate of one per year, they can be re-elected (§12(1–2)). It is a small, long-lived body and, given appropriate conditions in the broadcasting council, it can be dominated by one interest, that of the predominant party in the *Landtag*.

Only in relation to the programme advisory committee is there a reference to the socially relevant groups. This body has 20 members, one nominated by the *Land* government and the rest selected by the broadcasting council. The standing rules provide for 19 groups representing seven societal divisions to suggest three candidates each for membership; the broadcasting council selects from these and has the right, where a group does not make a recommendation, to appoint a candidate of its own choice. These members serve for six years and can be re-elected.

In electing the programme advisory committee, the broadcasting council acts as an electoral college chosen by the representatives of the public in the *Landtag* to do what the larger forum could not do and what the public at large could not do, namely to vet the candidates nominated by the socially relevant groups for their suitability to supervise the public broadcasting service. This would be an admirable arrangement, if the 'parliamentary subcommittee' (the broadcasting council) were then required to take a back seat and allow the direct representatives of the public at large to assume full responsibility for all but the purely administrative aspects of the work of the station. The latter task would fall to the other, similarly selected body, the administrative council, so that the broadcasting council would be a general supervisory body whose main task would be the election of its two aides; these would be responsible for the supervision of the day-to-day running of the station.

This interpretation of the role of the broadcasting council would find support in the frequency of the meetings of the respective bodies: the broadcasting council meets least frequently

[109]

(four times a year), with the programme advisory committee meeting about every two months and the administrative council approximately every month. The task assigned to the programme advisory committee (§18(1)) of advising the intendant 'in the whole area of the programmes of *Westdeutscher Rundfunk*, Cologne' would also suggest a key position close to the head of the station, who is required to attend its meetings – but it does not appoint him, the administrative council does.

The administrative council is less subordinate to the broadcasting council than the programme advisory committee: if the broadcasting council fails to elect a member, then the administrative council may itself make a choice; members can be removed from office by the broadcasting council, if the administrative council requests it to and after both bodies have discussed the case. The functions of the administrative council, compared with those of its SWF counterpart, are wide and include the following additional powers:

> §14 (1) The administrative council elects the intendant. The election requires confirmation by the broadcasting council.
>
> §14 (4) The administrative council supervises the station in its adherence to the guidelines for the programme (§4) and in its observation of the stipulations of §6. For this purpose it can in individual instances give the intendant instructions.

Thus this body emerges as the most powerful organ in the control structures; it is small, its members serve for seven years, it meets about once a month and *in camera*, it has full responsibility for supervising the management of the station and – a complete departure from the division of power exemplified in the other two stations – it holds considerable power in the field of programming, including the appointment of the intendant and the right to give him instructions in individual cases. Its approval is also required by the intendant for appointments to a considerable number of senior posts:

> the programme director, the directors of the administrative sections, the directors of the administrative sub-sections, the directors of the studios, the director of transmissions, the legal adviser, the technical directors (standing rules, §28 (3)).

The list is long and reaches down into the immediate areas where the programmes are made. The only senior appointment that the intendant can make without reference to the administrative council is in the case of a post 'with exclusively artistic duties' (law, §21(2) (e)). It is clearly intended that the administrative council should determine the pattern of activity in the station, including programming.

Of the three organs of control the one least close to the public is the most powerful, while the one closest to the public has no more than severely limited powers of advice. The most reliable check on abuse of power by the administrative council is the character of its members and the personality of the intendant, whose position is inherently weak. The *Land* government retains the right to exercise final supervision in individual cases where the law has been broken, but even this loses credibility when one considers the ease with which the ruling party in the *Landtag* could transmit its majority via the broadcasting council into the administrative council.

The unsatisfactory element in the parliamentary model is not so much the fact that the *Landtag* performs the first, basic selection of representatives; the weaknesses reside rather in the division of competence between the controlling bodies. The method by which representatives are selected for the three bodies is in itself satisfactory; what is questionable is the government's unwillingness to assign decisive power to the representatives of society, investing it instead in the body most likely to represent itself.

The NDR inter-*Land* agreement,[10] which postdates the WDR law by some nine months,[11] is very similar to its neighbour and, like it, very different from their common antecedent, the NWDR statute.[12] The break-up of the NWDR marked something of a turning-point in broadcasting history in West Germany; it was the beginning of obtrusive political involvement – witness the activities of the central government at the time, the attempts by the representatives of the supervisory bodies to gain a say in the running of the ARD and the characteristics of the broadcasting bodies which were subsequently founded.[13] The NDR compromise between three autonomous *Länder* has created a station which is even more closely linked to state executives and legislatures than WDR; NDR represents the most extreme constitutional submission to political influence in the Federal Republic.

The NDR controlling bodies are hardly larger than their WDR

counterparts (24:21, 8:7, 24:20) and yet each is divided to give each of the three *Länder* a share of representatives. In the broadcasting council the representatives of each of the *Länder* are further subdivided to give proportional representation to the parties as they stand in each parliament.

§8(2) outlines the formula for the broadcasting council:

The legislative bodies of the *Länder* elect the members of the broadcasting council for a period of 5 years according to the principle of proportional representation as follows: the *Land* Lower Saxony 12 members, the *Land* Schleswig-Holstein 6 members and the Free Hanseatic City of Hamburg 6 members. All members must have experience and knowledge in the field of broadcasting. Of the members for the *Land* Lower Saxony not more than 4, for the *Land* Schleswig-Holstein and for the Free Hanseatic City of Hamburg not more than 2 members each are to belong to the *Bundestag*, a *Landtag* or the *Bürgerschaft* (city parliament – AW).

For the administrative council §12(1) applies:

The administrative council consists of 8 members who are elected by the broadcasting council for a period of 5 years as follows: 4 members for the *Land* Lower Saxony and 2 members each from the *Land* Schleswig-Holstein and the Free Hanseatic City of Hamburg. Of the members of the administrative council not more than 4 may belong to the legislative bodies of the *Länder* or of the *Bund*.

In terms of direct parliamentary representation the maximum proportions are eight seats out of 24 in the broadcasting council, four out of eight in the administrative council and five out of 24 in the programme advisory committee – noticeably higher than in the corresponding WDR bodies with the exception possibly of the WDR administrative council for which no specification is laid down.

For the rest, there is little difference between the balance in WDR and in NDR. Two points only need to be noted in the present context: the power of the administrative council is less strong in NDR, and its approval is needed for a smaller number of senior posts in programme areas. A more significant singularity of the NDR constitution is that the intendant is elected by six out of eight votes (not by a simple majority) and is elected (normally) together with his deputy and for the same period of office – there is no arrangement for either of them to continue in office once tenure has expired, even if replacements have still to be found.[14]

The four stations illustrate the two main models of public control in their two main variations. Although the other stations conform to one pattern or the other to a greater or lesser extent, every station has inevitably its own peculiarities and all are worthy of study; of the rest perhaps SR (a combination of the two models which adds a parliamentary filter to the south German pluralistic model) and ZDF (introducing the added complexities of representation for the *Bund* and the *Länder* as well as for the socially relevant groups) are the two most interesting. The examples chosen are, however, sufficient to illustrate the way the system of controls works and the way small variations in concept and implementation change the nature of the link between the public and its broadcasting service. Public representation can be effective and strong close to the intendant in his programme duties, or it can be little more in practice than a necessary embellishment to protect the image of the station.

Finally, it must be noted that in the present chapter, as in the book generally, the concept under examination is public control and not the programme and its contents. The discussion is about control at the top and does not take account of the quality of programmes produced. An examination of the various programmes might suggest, revealing one of the paradoxes of the system, that the parliamentary model is to be preferred; it may be that parliamentary influence is a self-cancelling influence which leaves the broadcasters more scope to get on with the job of producing the programme.

CHANGES IN BAVARIA AND PUBLIC REACTIONS

A discussion of the models of control in broadcasting cannot now be complete without some reference to recent happenings in Bavaria. The full significance of these events has not yet become apparent, although it has not been and will not be ignored.

On 21 January 1972 the CSU majority introduced into the Bavarian *Landtag* a bill to change some parts of the law governing the Bavarian broadcasting service. Although they were initially successful and the amended law came into force on 1 March 1972, a storm of protest was unleashed which eventually became so powerful that most of the measures were reversed or modified. Constitutional lawyers would find material enough for several volumes if they were to explore to the full all the ramifications of the BR law case; its relevance here is that it lends perspective to a moment when, in the face of outspoken moves to adjust the balance of control in broadcasting, public and politicians alike developed a keen interest in and concern for the constitutional anchoring of broadcasting in the Federal Republic. Viewed in isolation, the reactions of the Bavarian public were aimed to stop the *Land* government interfering in broadcasting; in a wider context, they were a rejection of a change in the system in the direction of the north German model. There was also an associated reaction against a move towards commercial and private control of broadcasting, but it was particularly the increase in the influence of the political parties that was the focal point of attention. In this respect a turning-point was reached, for the action in Bavaria has proved to be a catalyst; there is evidence that the significance of the Bavarian symbol has been understood by the people in the best position to invest it with meaning elsewhere, the leaders of the political parties. There is as yet no evidence of corresponding action.

The sequence of events was as follows. In January 1972 the proposed changes to the law were introduced. After leaving the *Landtag* the bill was returned with a series of serious objections by the Bavarian senate, a unique and in this instance outstandingly wise second chamber. A massive opposition vote against the bill did not prevent its becoming law on 1 March. The first BR broadcasting council under the new law met for its constitutive sitting on 4 May 1972. By this time the SPD parliamentary party was ready to appeal to the Bavarian constitutional court and the forces of the public were being marshalled in support of two popular movements, whose object was to pressurize the government to permit a plebiscite[15] on the inclusion in the Bavarian constitution of clauses to protect public broadcasting from the influence of the political parties and to impose a ban on private broadcasting companies in Bavaria.

The action organized by the *Bürgerkomitee Rundfunkfreiheit* (citizens' committee for broadcasting freedom) quickly gathered support and submitted its proposal to the Bavarian Minister of the Interior. The latter's reactions were predictable: he doubted the constitutionality of the request for a plebiscite and also the legality and wisdom of a permanent constitutional ban on private broadcasting companies. The response of the Bavarian senate to the proposals was more interesting: it could not endorse the idea of the all-time ban, but it did endorse the attempt to stem the incursion of political forces into public territory; it even went so far as to publish its own, more moderate proposal (19 October 1972). The CSU majority, in desperation, pushed through the *Landtag* a counter-amendment to the constitution – without the necessary two-thirds majority. The latter move (14 December 1972) brought the second complaint of the SPD and the FDP to the constitutional court. The pressure from the opposition, the senate and the public could by now no longer be ignored; representatives of the three political parties and of the *Bürgerkomitee* met together in January 1973 and drew up a mutually acceptable draft for a modification to the constitution. This latter was approved by the *Landtag* with the necessary majority (8 May 1973) and eventually referred to the people of Bavaria for approval (1 July 1973). Once the result was known and the amendment to the constitution had entered the statute books, the new version of the BR law was introduced into the *Landtag* jointly by all three parties. It came into force on 1 August 1973.

The public voted firmly for the public, pluralistic control of broadcasting; the political parties (here the CSU majority) were given a clear rebuff for their meddling in what was strictly the province of society at large. The comparison with the *Spiegel* affair of 1962 is more than tempting; in both there was a happy coincidence of lucid informed leadership and youthful enthusiasm. The *Bürgerkomitee* was led by educationists, senior politicians, journalists and broadcasters; it heeded the advice of the 'upper house' and relied on youth and vigour for the action on the ground – it was mainly young people who collected some 90,000 signatures to give the movement its validity.

Let us now turn to the law and the proposed changes.

The original BR law[16] unambiguously encouraged pluralistic representation and control; a strong broadcasting council elected the intendant and its approval was required for his appointment of a deputy and of the senior broadcasting staff. All the necessary power to control the direction of the station's programme lay with the body representing the public.

One peculiarity of the original law was the inbuilt proportion of political to societal representatives on the broadcasting council. The socially relevant groups (listed in the law) had one seat each making a total of 28 and the other seats (usually 14) fell to the *Land* government (one), the senate (three) and the parliamentary parties at a rate of one seat per 25 members (or part), giving them together usually 10 seats. Members of the government could not represent the socially relevant groups, so that (ignoring the few members of the *Landtag* who might) not more than one-third of the seats could fall to political representatives.

The administrative council had three *ex officio* members: the president of the *Landtag*, the president of the senate and the president of the Bavarian administrative court, and four members elected by the broadcasting council who could not be members of that council, of the government or be under contract to BR.

The 'law to change the Bavarian broadcasting law' (1 March 1972)[17] made one major alteration in the regulations governing the composition of the broadcasting council: the parliamentary parties were to have one seat per 10 deputies (or part), giving them a total of about 21 seats; six additional societal groups were found to maintain a semblance of the original balance. The proportions became 25 directly political seats and 34 societal seats. Apart from increasing the already large body of 42 to almost ZDF proportions, the narrowing of the gap between the two types of representative effectively increased the importance of any party politicians selected to represent socially relevant groups. The second change introduced, which must be viewed in conjunction with the increase of political influence in the broadcasting council, was the extension of the range of appointments needing its approval into the immediate area of programming; such senior appointments would be given five-year contracts only – a factor which would further increase the hold of the broadcasting council over the work of the station. A chain of command was emerging through the new measures from the *Landtag* with its secure CSU majority into the programming sections of the station.

The Bavarian senate accepted the appropriateness of a review of the broadcasting law; it did not accept that there was a need to change it. It held the proposed changes to be potentially detrimental to the public system, and objected in particular to the three points outlined above.[18] On the changes in the broadcasting council, it had this to say:

> The rearrangement of the composition of the broadcasting council ... because of the increase in the number of members, makes the process of reaching opinions and decisions in the broadcasting council more difficult. The increased allocation of seats to deputies shifts the previous, balanced relationship to the socially relevant groups within the broadcasting council in the direction of increased influence by the parties and organs of state; thus it decreases in a constitutionally questionable manner the necessary distance of broadcasting and its organs from the state, which is demanded by the Federal Constitutional Court.

These arguments and the senate's claim that the incursion into the personnel field undermined the intendant's relationship with his staff as well as illegally restricting the latter's rights to job security, made no impression on the *Landtag* majority.

The goal of the citizens' committee was the inclusion in the Bavarian constitution of a new article (111a), which was rather more extreme than the senate's views:

> 1. Radio and television are operated exclusively by public institutions. The stations are supervised by a broadcasting council ... The participation of the state government, the senate and the *Landtag* may not exceed one-third.[19]

The formula for parliamentary members was to be one per 20 deputies (or part), a very minor modification of the original law.

The modified view of the senate as it was publicized in October 1972 did not make broadcasting exclusively an activity for public corporations, but it did endorse public control in a most subtle formulation:

> Broadcasting may only be practised in full accountability to the public. The institutions, no matter what their legal form, must be so organized that all groups which can be considered relevant to society can have an influence in the collegial organs and get a hearing in the overall programme.[20]

By the time the three parties and the representatives of the citizens' committee had had time to digest this and to discuss a mutually acceptable solution, the formulation had become subtle in the extreme. The text agreed for the new article 111a[21] contains a

definition of broadcasting and its role in society and continues
with a charter of public control:

> 2. Broadcasting is practised in public accountability and within the
> purview of public law. An appropriate share in the supervision of
> broadcasting is to be given to all political, confessional and social
> groups which can be considered significant. The share of the
> representatives sent by the state government, the *Landtag* and the
> senate to the supervisory bodies may not exceed one-third. The
> confessional and social groups elect or appoint their representatives
> themselves.

The 'Bavarian model' had been established; the principle of
public control secured in a two-thirds share of the broadcasting
council seats had entered the statute books – and at the people's
behest. At the same time the one-third limit on political seats
was becoming a ubiquitous formula among the theorists of
broadcasting.

Another significant aspect of the events in Bavaria was emphasized by a CSU spokesman who read out a prepared statement to
the *Landtag* during the discussion of the plebiscite. The seventh
point in the paper is the most relevant here; it indicates the wider
import of the people's victory:

> 7. The discussion of broadcasting policies in the last few years
> initiated by the CSU has intensified the attention of the population
> on questions of media policy. This should ensure the plebiscite
> appropriate participation and will give the freedom of opinion the
> protection which only the critical attention of the public also in
> respect of the mass media can secure.[22]

It would have been interesting and instructive to observe the
reactions of the *Landtag* when this point was read to it; however,
the CSU's remarks do raise an issue of importance and do contain
a great truth: the final guarantee of free public broadcasting is the
watchfulness of the public; there is no substitute for its critical
attention.

The CSU certainly engendered an uncommon degree of active
public interest, and it was not restricted to the people of Bavaria
– reactions were recorded in almost all areas of the Federal
Republic, including even some north German CDU circles. What
the CSU paper does not disclose is how this critical interest can
be created and maintained when there are no immediate crises to

fight. The discussion in the next chapter will show how little public reaction there is elsewhere to ingrained political abuses in the control of broadcasting. The active involvement of the public at large has been provoked as yet only by the one direct assault on its sense of freedom; it remains to be seen whether this aspect of the Bavarian case will appear in future as merely a moment of passing fury, or as a first awakening of public awareness.

CHAPTER EIGHT

The Political Invasion of Public Broadcasting

If the West German broadcasting stations continue to produce and transmit a generally high level of programme, it is in spite of the efforts of the political parties to influence them in their work. The struggle between the parties to gain the upper hand in individual stations has been contested with increasing openness and decreasing respect for the ethics of public life. The manner in which the political parties have on occasion conducted themselves is evidence of the immaturity that persists in political life in the Federal Republic. This chapter in the history of West German broadcasting is a sad one, and one on which the final word cannot yet be written. Although there are signs of change in the thinking and attitudes of political leaders, they exist mainly in documents which are no more than statements of intent. All the indications are that many of the politicians involved in the control of broadcasting, and they are mainly senior politicians, choose to forget that broadcasting is a public prerogative; they seem to regard their responsibilities in this sector as delimited by party-political allegiance and react to criticism (largely by ignoring it) as if that sector of their activities were beyond public scrutiny. Nor has the public acted as yet to prove to them that it is not. If our objective were to prove that in some respects West German leaders still regard themselves as a breed apart, then we could seek no better medium to view them through than broadcasting.

The discussion that follows is an examination of some of the facts that have emerged in recent years which highlight the activities of the parties in the supervisory bodies of the broadcasting stations. Evidence of contraventions of broadcasting laws, of the blocking of the work of the stations, of the sharing out on a political basis of senior appointments and also of posts directly in programming areas will be called to illustrate the extent of the party-political invasion of public broadcasting. The sources used as a basis for this investigation are all published,[1] and the evidence has been made available to the German public; confidential information available to the present writer, although it fully substantiates the picture that will emerge below, will not be quoted. It is not the task of the present work to amass new evidence to add to the already substantial supply, nor is it its task to present an exhaustive account of events to date; here a development will be depicted in outline in those areas where it is most obvious, the danger of a political subversion of public rights will be shown to be real and the consequent need for action against it (by broadcasters and public) explained.

THE SUPERVISORY BODIES

It is never possible in the final analysis to say what the extent of political representation in the supervisory bodies is. Not all seats available to legislatures and executives are always allocated to practising politicians, not all practising politicians on the supervisory bodies (whether they represent legislature, executive or society) will always act as members of a political group, and not all members of the supervisory bodies who are not practising politicians can be relied upon never to act as members of a political group. It is thus not a particularly useful exercise to analyse membership lists and count off seats in terms of right and left; it is, however, instructive to take those laws that set a specific limit on the number of parliamentary seats in a given organ, where this limit is known to have been overstepped, and examine the nature of the infringement.

A contravention of the written law can be quoted in the two north German stations constituted according to the parliamentary model – NDR and WDR. The limits set here are: NDR, eight members only of the broadcasting council and four of the administrative council; WDR, four members of the broadcasting council and no stated limit on parliamentary membership of the administrative council.

The WDR aberration illustrates the importance the political parties attach to strong representation in the stations. The broadcasting council was constituted correctly in late February 1970; later in the year (14 June) *Landtag* elections were held and a shift of emphasis occurred: in addition to the existing members, two further members of the broadcasting council were returned as deputies, making a total of six.[2] This shows that members of supervisory bodies other than elected politicians stand very high in party rankings and thus that non-membership of a legislative body says nothing for party-political neutrality; it does not offer evidence of a deliberate breach of the law. The case against the six would have been proven if they had persisted in their membership of the broadcasting council. They did not. Since that time the law has been meticulously observed.

Although no limits exist for the administrative council, it should perhaps be noted in passing that six of its seven members have for years been senior politicians.

The NDR situation was and is different. In 1969 the broadcasting council already had a dozen parliamentarians among its members, in 1970 the number rose to 15 and in 1973 to 16; where the maximum proportion of elected politicians should not exceed one-third, the actual proportion had become two-thirds. There can be no claim of ignorance or accident on the part of the politicians involved and the parties nominating them; moreover the practice of ignoring the law is well-established in all three NDR *Länder*.

The representatives of each *Land* are chosen by the parties who, in theory, put forward lists of candidates for election by the relevant parliament; the process has become a political battle in which the parties submit exactly the number of names they would be proportionally entitled to, virtually forcing the hand of the legislative assembly. Herbert Janssen, a keen observer of party tactics in broadcasting, analysed[3] the 1970 elections to the broadcasting council to show the following pattern of nominations: Lower Saxony (12 seats), CDU six and SPD six with each offering three elected politicians (six elected politicians with four permitted); Hamburg (six), CDU two deputies, SPD two deputies out of three nominations, and FDP one deputy (five elected politicians with a permitted total of two) – the FDP seat was conceded to it by the SPD from its proportional share of four. In

Schleswig-Holstein (six) the CDU tried to alter the established proportions by offering four instead of three names (two deputies), while the SPD put forward its 'correct' share of three names (all deputies). The *Landtag* was 'forced' to make a selection and the CDU tactic paid dividends (four elected politicians and not five joined the broadcasting council, although two is the permitted limit). The public's political representatives thus blatantly deny the public its right to control the broadcasting service.

This is the most overt exhibition of lawbreaking in the system. It is tolerated probably because to challenge the situation would mean challenging the parliaments in the administrative courts and possibly in the Federal Constitutional Court, when there is a lack of clarity about how and by whom this could be done, and because, in any case, the all-powerful body is the administrative council and the rules there are carefully observed – at least in terms of numbers.

The NDR administrative council is the supervisory body which has occasioned most comment in the Federal Republic in the recent past. In the article just quoted, Janssen reported that the parliamentary parties in Lower Saxony had coupled recommendations for the administrative council with their nominations for the broadcasting council (CDU: Willy Weber, Dr Werner Remmers; SPD: Dr Hans Schmidt, Martin Neuffer) as had the CDU in Hamburg (Jürgen Echternach). It is difficult to believe that this does not happen elsewhere, perhaps less openly. The same names appear in the list of elected administrative council members,[4] so the members of the broadcasting council did as they were bidden; the membership of the administrative council was determined by the political parties in the *Länder* on the basis of a proportional carve-up. It is possible that the men chosen were the best candidates for the job (Martin Neuffer is now NDR intendant); it is more likely that the members of the broadcasting council, most of them party stalwarts and a significant number party chairmen and deputy-chairmen, chose to obey party directives to preserve the proportions – thus breaking the rule which, without exception, appears in every broadcasting law in the Federal Republic: members are not bound by outside directives in the execution of their duties as members of the broadcasting council. This one example amply illustrates the weakness of the parliamentary model: the public interest and even the standing of parliaments are easily sacrificed to party-political infighting. From this example it can be seen where the real problem lies, where the problem of West German political life might lie. If the members of the supervisory bodies fail in their constitutional duty, then the system cannot work. When public representatives are no more than spokesmen for political groups, then no amount of legislation, no electoral safeguards will uphold the freedom of broadcasting. The individual's regard for his own freedom is the vital factor, particularly when he is so close to the state government. The very people who should seek to serve the ideal of personal and public freedom, the political leaders, are here seen to lack the essential democratic will; they see their own importance only in terms of service to the political system in its crudest form.

THE 'FRIENDS' OF BROADCASTING

Party-political interference with the substance of public broadcasting is not merely an intermittent phenomenon associated with the election of supervisory bodies; there is a constant pressure on members of broadcasting supervisory bodies and, in some cases, of production teams to be guided in their decisions by at least party preferences. On the fringes of some stations a number of pressure groups called *Freundeskreise* (circles of friends) are a permanent institution. The black humour of the name may be totally unintentional – they are certainly nobody's friends. These groups, usually leading politicians, meet regularly to discuss matters relating to broadcasting; members of the supervisory bodies are usually present and sometimes important members of broadcasting staff. They function almost as outer cabinets, helping colleagues within the stations to reach the right policy decisions.

The *Freundeskreise* are most often associated with ZDF where, in the evening before every sitting of the television council,

> the members who have the task of supervising the station repair to the party annexes to receive their orders. Divided up into red and black the company assembles in two circles: the CDU/CSU group in the Mainz CDU parliamentary party's hall on the *Deutschhausplatz*, the SPD group in the party's own *Rheinhessenhof* ...[5]

Because of their party orientation they are, as Michael Schmid-Ospach puts it, 'an easy down-payment of a two-party system in broadcasting'.[6] Their activities effectively close the gap between the basically pluralistic ZDF and the parliamentary WDR and NDR:

> When, as with ZDF, every important television council decision is debated in advance by the CDU and SPD *Freundeskreise*, when party discipline is not only expected but is also demonstrably observed, then the difference between the social groups, pluralistic system and the parliamentary, political system is reduced to procedural formalities.[7]

It is no coincidence that the phenomenon of the *Freundeskreise* is linked most closely with ZDF, for it was here that the practice seems to have originated. When the first television council was unable to agree about procedures for electing the intendant, party-political groups were formed whose unofficial discussions linked a solution here with a formula by which posts within the station were allocated – without naming individual personnel – in equal sets to each group.[8] Since then the *Freundeskreise* have continued to function, pre-empting important decisions of the television council. To influence the business of the council one has to be a member of one of the groups, which unlike those of WDR and NDR, embrace station staff as well as members of the supervisory bodies. It is already a negation of the principles of public broadcasting for the question of influence to be reduced to a question of membership of a party-political group; when the decisions influenced by these groups take in appointments and programming, the situation becomes grave in the extreme.

There are other ways of looking at the activities of the *Freundeskreise*. A practical view was revealed in a public exchange of letters between two representatives of the churches, Dr Johannes Niemeyer (Roman Catholic representative on the ZDF television council) and Robert Geisendörfer (Protestant special observer on television affairs).[9] Without denying his worries about the system, Dr Niemeyer took a strongly realistic view:

> The thorny business of public supervision has its own necessities. Without the *Freundeskreise* the forces in society would be within the bounds of legality, but without any real influence. In the *Freundeskreise* they have at least the possibility of joining in with some weight when the decisions on the various questions are reached, and of fulfilling their responsibilities.

His view is similar to that expounded somewhat earlier by Dr Friedrich Zimmermann, a *Bundestag* deputy and chairman of the CDU/CSU working party on broadcasting, who described broadcasting as an eminently political activity which cannot be usefully 'de-politicized'; thus

> the preparatory bodies of the parties or political groups in the individual stations, the so-called *Freundeskreise*, are absolutely necessary – just as the parties' working parties in the *Landtage* and the *Bundestag* are necessary – to prepare the real work of the plenary body.[10]

Dr Zimmermann saw the *Freundeskreis* as a necessary tool in a political situation, Dr Niemeyer regarded it as a necessary evil. The latter's partner in the epistolary debate, although he valued legality higher than influence, did not go so far as to suggest that the *Freundeskreise* were unnecessary or should be banned. Geisendörfer suggested a new circle of friends made up solely of representatives of the socially relevant groups. This third circle, the 'grey' circle, would, he suggested, have considerable influence and ought to be given serious thought. His efforts were not totally vain, for some time later his erstwhile controvertist, Dr Niemeyer, was reported as seeking support to break the hold of CDU and SPD.[11] However, the third group has not materialized, and the CDU and SPD groups are as strong as ever; it seems that *Freundeskreise*, useful or not, will remain a feature of the broadcasting landscape in Mainz, Cologne and Hamburg for the foreseeable future.

Before leaving this section, a development which the present writer does not pretend to understand must be noted. Under amusing and intriguing circumstances the WDR broadcasting council chose, in May 1974, to ignore all the names suggested to it by the SPD for membership of the WDR programme advisory committee. Many of the societal groups had, it seems, tried their hand at the game so often indulged in by the parties; 11 of them suggested one name only, leaving the SPD with one seat out of the 19. The SPD *Land* government, to cap the situation, selected for its statutory seat, not a senior party member but a much respected journalist, Dr Joachim Besser. Unwittingly democracy seemed to have triumphed; a final twist came when, correctly, Dr

[126]

Besser refused the seat on the grounds that he was often employed by WDR in his capacity as a journalist.[12]

It is much too soon to draw any conclusions from the action in this isolated instance of the socially relevant groups and of the broadcasting council; a little gentle speculation about a change towards active pluralism will be permissible, if and when the pattern is repeated in WDR or elsewhere.

SOME EFFECTS OF POLARIZATION

When polarization on party-political fronts threatened to stop the ZDF television council functioning, the solution was found outside it in an 'institutionalized' apportionment of staff posts. There are other examples which show that party-political polarization inside and outside supervisory bodies can bring their work to a complete standstill; indeed it can, for a time, prevent the constitution even of these bodies.

In 1972 the political manœuvring over the membership of the ZDF administrative council became so involved that its full complement of elected members was finally determined some days after it was legally due to take up its work. Michael Schmid-Ospach has analysed this particular situation[13] and, although he somewhat overstates his case, his commentary throws light on the way control and supervision in public broadcasting can so readily devolve to the legislative bodies.

In 1972 the problem arose because the SPD had been making electoral gains and had assumed the majority in the conference of the prime ministers of the *Länder* (6:5), which has the task of electing three members of the administrative council. The composition of the latter was at the time five CDU (three elected by the television council and two by the prime ministers), three SPD (two, one) and one FDP (representing the federal government). With their new majority in the conference, the SPD could now hope to take two of the three seats falling to the prime ministers. However, they could pull off the coup (making the balance 4:4:1) only if the CDU-dominated television council did not compensate in its allocation of seats. The timing of the two parts of the election was thus of the essence: the last to elect its members could hope to decide the final balance in the administrative council – the FDP member could be expected to vote with the representatives of the FDP's coalition partner in Bonn.

[127]

This analysis is in itself a revealing commentary on the sort of thinking that goes into the making of broadcasting supervisory bodies. The outcome of the ZDF election revealed even more machinations. The election left the composition of the administrative council unchanged, in return for which concession the SPD seems to have gained an appointment within the station (administrative director) and a promise in a letter from prime minister Kohl (CDU, Rhineland-Palatinate) to prime minister Kühn (SPD, North Rhine-Westphalia) that the CDU would vacate one of its seats on the council by the end of 1973 in favour of the SPD. This would create the 4:4:1 balance desired by the SPD, but leave the majority ultimately dependent on the outcome of the *Bundestag* elections and the shape of the coalition in Bonn. Michael Schmid-Ospach, in reporting the existence of the letter,[14] felt that the SPD had struck a poor bargain in accepting a post within the station instead of taking control (for the first time) of the administrative council. At the end of 1973, however, Dr Walter Gammert stepped down in favour of Klaus Schütz, so the criticism has lost some of its validity. The move also shows how the question of control in ZDF (which is only one, albeit an outstanding example) is decided absolutely and exclusively between the two major parties.

The more important the area in which a decision is to be made, the greater and the more blatant the party-political polarization and interference; and no post is more crucial in a broadcasting station than that of intendant. The election or re-election of an intendant is certain to bring journalistic activity to fever pitch, and the events surrounding these elections are often sufficiently bizarre to warrant the attention they receive.

In two recent re-elections (ZDF, WDR) speculation was encouraged by the fact that the question of the appointment was in each case raised long before the expiry of the incumbent's period of office. Professor Holzamer was, for example, re-elected in February 1971 for his third period of office which commenced in March 1972. Although Klaus von Bismarck was re-elected at the correct time, the discussion of the appointment started several months before. In both cases the reason for the early interest was the fact that senior members of staff were approaching retirement age: Professor Holzamer himself in ZDF and Professor Brack in WDR.

Professor Holzamer's re-election was effected before his sixty-fifth birthday; by 1977 when his present period of office expires he will be approaching 71. It seems certain that this will be his last period of office. The significance of his early re-election seems to be that, apart from avoiding any wrangles about the time of his birthday when a failure to re-elect him would have thrust him ungracefully into retirement, it gave the CDU the assurance that a man of its choice would be the head of the station over a period of apparent transition. At the time of the election a change to an SPD choice might have been justified by the general political scene, but it was far from clear that this climate would hold. Had the CDU ousted the SPD in 1972 (or 1973, the expected date) then they would have conceded nothing to the SPD in ZDF; even though they lost the election, they retained control of a key post for at least the duration of the new SPD administration. The SPD could try to reverse the situation by forcing an early replacement of Professor Holzamer before the next federal elections – 1976 will be a fascinating year to observe in West Germany.

Professor Brack held two posts in WDR, that of legal adviser and that of administrative director, in the latter capacity with supervision of the station's finances. His retirement opened up the possibility of a bi- or even tripartite division of these areas of responsibility. By advancing the discussion of the next intendant the parties in the administrative council could hope to balance out between them three or four important posts. The motives for the early moves were hardly to ease von Bismarck's mind, indeed he was kept waiting for a decision until January 1971; nor were the parties' efforts rewarded – Professor Brack's posts were divided into two only and von Bismarck was re-elected.

An intendant who is appointed in a situation in which a party carve-up of posts is more important than his personal qualities, cannot be confident in his professional claims to the job. The other circumstances of von Bismarck's re-election could only undermine his position further. There were constant rumours in 1970 that the SPD was seeking other candidates and would nominate von Bismarck only if the CDU would also back him as a neutral candidate, i.e. the post would not be counted against the SPD allocation. The voting, in fact, was 4:3,[15] so that the CDU did not concede this point. Von Bismarck has the pleasure of knowing that he is something of a moderate; but with what must be seen as half-hearted support from the people who elected him, he must feel fundamentally insecure.

Von Bismarck's first re-election in 1965 had been a painless matter, but his original appointment had followed a series of abortive attempts to elect other people which makes the 1970 manœuvrings seem civilized by comparison:

> The administrative council, after repeated adjournments, had twice re-elected the outgoing intendant, Hanns Hartmann, whose period of office ended on 31 December 1960, in crucial votes by 4:3. Twice the broadcasting council refused its confirmation ... Then Dr Dieter Sattler (CDU) declined the post after he had been elected by three votes with three abstentions and one member absent, because he felt that the majority was not viable. Only on 16 December 1960 did the administrative council elect von Bismarck unanimously by six votes with one member absent. The whole process took from 6 October until 21 December. Von Bismarck took up office on 4 April 1961. WDR was without an intendant for three months.[16]

Whatever the reasons for the lack of agreement in 1960, it manifested itself as an altercation between the broadcasting council and the administrative council; even if it was politically motivated it remained refreshingly legitimate – and although the election was late, the station was never without a legal head. And the 1970 stalemate did not reach the stage where it constituted a legal problem. This peculiar distinction must go to NDR where, in 1973, the administrative council failed to elect the intendant by the constitutional deadline; the station was left without a properly appointed legal head and the broadcasting council had not even been involved.

The total deadlock in the latest NDR intendant election will, perhaps, emerge as the extreme case in the trend in the West German broadcasting stations towards polarization; whether it marks the end of the phase is as yet impossible to say. The behaviour of the NDR administrative council when the question of the election of the intendant was raised was not new, it remained all too clearly in character; the events of late 1973 and early 1974 provide only an extreme example of typical NDR administrative council tactics whenever subjects involving the standing of one or other of the two sides are tabled for discussion.

A less recent example can be quoted to set the scene; it was reported in *Funk-Korrespondenz* under the title: 'Walk-out again makes NDR administrative council inquorate.'[17]

At its meeting on 27 March the administrative council of the *Norddeutscher Rundfunk* was unable to complete five of the agenda tabled, because after two hours of discussion it was made inquorate by the withdrawal of three of its SPD members.

Following their normal practice the CDU members issued an explanatory statement – as did the SPD. Only a short time before the situation had been reversed – the CDU had walked out. It was clearly a tit-for-tat situation; although the real reason for the SPD sabotage on this occasion might have been less the personnel decisions they avoided than the two agenda points mentioned at the end of the *Funk-Korrespondenz* report: a CDU complaint that an SPD candidate in the Schleswig-Holstein *Landtag* elections was receiving particularly favourable treatment in NDR programmes, and a CDU proposal that the administrative council should set up its own standing programme committee.

It was in this sort of atmosphere that these same people (one member only had changed in the intervening period) failed to set about the task of electing an intendant in 1973. The election had to be completed by 6 November 1973, when the period of office of the then incumbent was to end; the first attempt to elect his successor was made on 24 September 1973 and the new intendant was finally elected on 18 February 1974. The facts speak for themselves.

The date set for the election of the NDR intendant is particularly important because the period of office of both the intendant and his deputy ends on the same day and the law contains no regulation to cover the eventual need for an interregnum. In failing to appoint a successor to the intendant by the date set, the members of the administrative council laid themselves open to a charge of dereliction of duty; the period that elapsed before the situation was remedied is a monumental testimony to the total impoverishment of democracy in West German broadcasting at the hands of the political parties. *Der Spiegel* did not mince its words in an article published the day before Schröder's period of office ended:

The commotion is about more than just a leadership crisis in NDR. It is true that the politicians have contravened a broadcasting law by not electing the intendants in time. But the scandal is more serious still, because it shows that the state (governments and parliaments) have handed broadcasting over to politicians – against the word and the spirit of the constitution.[18]

'Scandal' was a word on many lips during the 15 weeks when the station was without a legal head; even more scandalous perhaps is the apparent total absence of consequences for the members of the administrative council. There have been no resignations and no motions of censure outside the media; nothing has been done to remedy the situation for the future.

There have been no consequences, but the charge of dereliction of duty applies in the final analysis only to the administrative council; it cannot be laid at the feet of the final instance of supervision, the three *Länder*. Action was taken during the period between November and February and, in a sense, it was adequate and went to the limit reasonable for the state in its dealings with public broadcasting. The question of final legal supervision by the state is an extremely difficult one; the nature of this office is not understood even by the legal experts, although it is taken generally to be the power to remind the stations of their duty – beyond this is mystery. In the case in hand the mystery goes deeper; NDR has three final instances which seem, like the parties, afraid that one might steal a march on the others.[19]

On 14 November 1973 a letter was sent to the NDR administrative council by the head of the State Chancellery in Schleswig-Holstein – with the agreement of the other two *Länder*. The wording is careful to a nicety:

> The supervising governments of the *Länder* which are party to the inter-*Land* agreement point out that the election of the new intendant and of his deputy ... had to be completed by 6 November 1973. The administrative council has not met this legal obligation.
>
> The *Land* governments therefore entreat the administrative council ... to complete the election of the intendants forthwith. The *Land* governments reserve the right to take further supervisory measures, if an election has not been held by 31 December 1973, and the functioning of the station makes this seem imperative.[20]

The final phrase is most important: it is a reservation, a let-out for the governments; it is also a perfectly valid assessment of the moment when active intervention might become necessary. In this instance it did not become necessary, for the station continued to function; in fact, the letter itself contained the information that the longest-serving director was to be delegated to supervise NDR affairs until a new intendant was appointed. Having thus secured the ability of the station to function, the State Chancellery had absolved itself from any need to prosecute further the problem of the administrative council's inability to act. Whether it should allow the matter to pass completely without review is a question that cannot be answered here.

One point must be emphasized: the intervention of the state, and it was this, was carried out simply and unobtrusively without a hint of 'state control'; the administrative council was helped out of a self-imposed impossible position with an application of commonsense that could not have been anything but surprising. The system, in the end, proved flexible enough for the vital business of public broadcasting to continue unimpeded through the crisis – in spite of the inadequacies of the law and in spite of the shortsightedness of the political parties. The appointment of the senior director as a *locum tenens* was, additionally, an object lesson for the administrative council in practical problem-solving: he was chosen according to totally impartial and generally acceptable criteria untainted by party proportionalism. The State Chancellery established something of what could be termed the sanity of normal practice and helped the parties out of their almost permanent vicious circle of growing incompetence.

These marginally encouraging features, however, in no way contradict the general impression given of the system by the elections of intendants in the north German stations; an adequate summing-up is provided by the title of an article by Theodor Eschenburg which must speak for the attitude of many commentators: *Proporzbrunst und Schlammperei*.[21] It is untranslatable but can be rendered roughly as: Ruttish Proportionalism and Sloppy Neglect.

As a footnote it should, perhaps, be recorded that Gerhard Schröder, whom the NDR administrative council was at pains not to re-elect and who was replaced by Martin Neuffer, was elected intendant of neighbouring station *Radio Bremen* on 3 July 1974.

THE PARTIES AND THE APPOINTMENT OF SENIOR PERSONNEL

Throughout the above sections it has been suggested that the political parties attempt to acquire territory in the broadcasting stations by ensuring that appointees to important posts are of an acceptable party colouring. It is not possible ultimately to measure the effect of this practice: what a broadcaster conveys through his programme may have quite the opposite effect to that intended; often the influence of the political forces in the stations achieves only a negative moderation of programme content rather than a positive statement in keeping with a recognizable party line. The present writer holds the view that the case that political influence is a decisive factor in the programme is not proven, except in a few obvious instances which have attracted the interest of the press. Nevertheless, there is strong evidence to indicate that the party representatives on the supervisory bodies believe that securing acceptable senior personnel is important; if the programmes do not reflect the apportionment of posts between them more obviously, it is not their fault. For this reason it is important in the present context to look more closely at the business of political apportionment.

Sir Hugh Carleton Greene, perhaps the Englishman with the most knowledge and understanding of the West German broadcasting system, made the following comment in a television programme on the situation in West German broadcasting:

> It is a scandal that an intendant or a deputy can be elected or not elected – not because of his personal qualities and experience, but because he is acceptable or unacceptable to the CDU or the SPD.[22]

He was referring to the outstanding election of the NDR intendant and his remarks should probably be seen rather in the light of the person not elected than as a comment on the intendant-to-be. In this context his words were most apposite. Schröder's name was submitted and a vote taken at a meeting held on 16 November 1973. The result was a 4:4 stalemate,[23] a clear indication of a party-line vote. The question of the deputy intendant, which was to have been decided at the same meeting, was then left open. Schröder and his deputy represented SPD and CDU respectively and thus constituted a package acceptable to both sides; once one fell into disfavour both were lost (neither would gain the necessary six votes). A decision on the deputy before one on the intendant would have meant the concession of the intendant to the other side. The same idea of a package also applied, as we have seen, to WDR and is an institution in ZDF; it is not surprising that the press talks of CDU and SPD posts and, when these look as if they will change hands, of takeover bids.

Three of the concise, headline paragraphs used by *Der Spiegel* to indicate the subject of its articles provide an interesting comment on the way party manœuvrings for broadcasting posts can be interpreted; they are chosen because they refer to different stations:

(a) To 'get its claws' on ZDF, the CDU is making use of its influence in the administrative council: important staff posts are being filled with CDU sympathizers.
(b) After the occupation of *Bayerischer Rundfunk* and the infiltration of ZDF, the CDU now wants to seize power in WDR.
(c) The CDU now wants to get its hands on the sole SPD bastion in *Saarländischer Rundfunk*, director for radio programmes.[24]

All attack the CDU (a *Spiegel* pastime), but none quite so strongly as the preamble to the full-scale article on ZDF of 4 October 1971:

In time for the 1973 federal elections ZDF is to become a CDF, a Christian Democratic Union station. The CDU is attempting to fill the key positions with devoted party supporters, it is outsmarting the SPD in the supervisory bodies and has the intendant on a lead. To stop the Union's advance the SPD, out of luck in broadcasting politics, is even considering the termination of the ZDF inter-*Land* agreement.[25]

Even through the misrepresentation of the idea that the SPD as such could secede from an agreement between the *Länder* and the bitter criticism of the CDU, a glimmer of the truth of the situation shines through: the SPD is not so much innocent of manipulation as inept at it.

In many ways 1971 was a year of the parties, with the interest of the press stimulated by the idea that the CDU was shoring up its weakened political position by preparing the ground for a triumphant return to power via the broadcasting media. Gerhard

Schröder, then chairman of the ARD, noticed the increasing interest of the parties in the posts lower down the broadcasting hierarchy and commented on it in his review of the year 1971. His remarks would hardly have won him the approbation of the politicians in his own administrative council:

> Similarly, 1971 brought attempts at the clarification and settlement of misunderstandings in the relationship between the political parties and the societal groups in respect of the broadcasting stations, yet essentially it was the efforts to extend the possibilities of influencing the work of the production teams and supervisory bodies that were predominant; the parties began to compete with each other in such a way that the dangers of proportional solutions were greatly increased at all levels in the work of broadcasting. Within the parties media policy was largely understood no longer as politics for the media, with the objective of maintaining that area of freedom which is indispensable for the freedom of information and opinion, but as politics with the media and into the media with the objective of enlisting them for their respective self-portrayal.[26]

The parties were beginning to extend the range of their influence down into the areas in the stations where the programmes are made. Something of this was stressed by Heiko Flottau when he discussed the unexpectedly early renewal of the contract of Joseph Viehöver, programme director and deputy intendant of ZDF, in April 1973. The deputy intendant was the SPD balance for the CDU intendant, so that SPD tactics seemed to be the reason for the renewal of a contract that would now run until 1980. The move led Flottau to comment on the apportioning of posts lower down the hierarchy and to introduce a remark made by an SPD spokesman: 'I am assuming that the studio in Brussels cannot be occupied totally without consultation with the SPD'; Flottau adds: 'Nothing proves more clearly than this sentence that party-political apportionment is slowly spreading from the tops of the stations into the middle strata.'[27]

A few months after the renewal of his contract Viehöver was taken ill and died; many old questions were reopened as the search for a replacement got under way. Again the commentators saw fit to criticize the spread of political influence into programming posts. Wolf Donner, writing in *Die Zeit*, was quite alarmist:

> Germany's telegods sit in Bonn, not in the stations. Slowly but surely state broadcasting is establishing itself here after the repulsive

example of the French ORTF. For a long time now the demand for balance has been spreading from the programme into the personnel structures of the stations, for a long time now the parties have been tinkering with the middle echelons and no longer just at the top: at the level of correspondents, departmental heads and *Land* studio directors ...[28]

The comparison with ORTF cannot be taken seriously, but what cannot be ignored is the point made by both Donner and Flottau that the parties were beginning to see that influence at the top was not sufficient to produce the desired effects in the programme. It was becoming increasingly obvious that the parties were trying to achieve results in the message reaching the public through the media – they were beginning to attack the foundations of the public system.

This more direct interference by the political parties in the business of programming constituted an encroachment upon the rights of the individual programme staff as well as upon those of the public, and the broadcasters have reacted in their own way to the pressure on them. It must be clear before moving on to this closely related aspect of broadcasting that the two developments cannot be viewed diachronically only, for as the broadcasters' action can be related to political pressure, so also can the intensification of party-political activity, particularly by CDU and CSU, be interpreted as an attempt to consolidate in the face of unfavourable treatment in the programmes. This, however, does not in any way justify a development that hits at the essence of public broadcasting; indeed, one can see the broadcasters as the sensitive point in the system where the attack is first noted and the first reactions recorded. The public is the final line of defence before the Constitutional Court; so far, however, the broadcasters have chosen to fight for their liberty within the system, they have not used their undoubted power of appeal to the public. The public has so far remained singularly unaware of the struggle that has been in progress for almost half a decade for the most fundamental of its basic rights.

❦

CHAPTER NINE

The Freedom of Broadcasting—
An Internal Problem

No movement in the history of West German broadcasting has been the cause of so much controversy and misunderstanding, or has caused so much fear among senior broadcasters and politicians as the movement of the broadcasting journalists within the stations to establish various statutes designed to give them certain guarantees in the execution of their public task. Although the broadcasting journalists took great pains to illuminate the objectives of the movement for internal broadcasting freedom (*innere Rundfunkfreiheit*), the general tendency has been to ignore or lose sight of these. The present phase in the broadcasters' movement, as in West German broadcasting generally, is one of interim solutions based on uncertainty rather than on understanding. Otto Wilfert, a member of ZDF programme staff devoted to the cause of the internal securing of freedom, reported from a seminar organized by the Radio-Television-Film-Union[1] that even in May 1974 there was nothing to indicate clarity of vision:

> The ideas about how and where representation for production staff with their special problems should be established were as confused as they were five years ago at the beginning of the so-called statutes movement.[2]

It would hardly be just to the broadcasters' ideals simply to establish what the objectives of the movement were and how far they have been achieved. Much of the importance of the movement derives from misreadings of it and the related reactions. It is too early to say whether the movement has carried the understanding of the freedom of broadcasting to a new level. It is clear to the present writer that the way the broadcasters themselves approach fundamental issues, given the situation in the Federal Republic as outlined above, does introduce a new dimension of considerable importance, which the system, in the long term, will have to face – except the forces threatening the external freedom of broadcasting recant and withdraw. One can expect that the debate about the meaning and seat of freedom, of democratic pluralism in broadcasting, will continue.

What follows does not pretend to be a full account of all the ramifications of the movement;[3] its place in the general system of co-determination and personnel representation, its relation to the trade union movement and of the latter to the broadcasting services are, for example, aspects that cannot be explored here. Here the main concern is to show that the staff who produce the programmes in the stations had become aware of an area in the system which had previously not been defined, but which was the point where their freedom had to be guaranteed.

THE STATUTES MOVEMENT

In their comments on the status of the intendant, the members of the Michel Commission referred indirectly to the statutes movement (then quite new) and in so doing revealed three aspects of the commonest approach to the question of internal broadcasting freedom which constituted a misapprehension of the broadcasters' position:

> (It would be) questionable under constitutional law to grant journalist colleagues a right to have a say in the planning of the programme which would be binding on the intendant ... The democratic legitimation of the intendant as a monocratic executive organ is guaranteed in his responsibility to the broadcasting council, which for its part represents the society in which broadcasting is founded.[4]

The movement is seen in relation to the position of the intendant and as an attack on this position; the whole question is related to the written constitutions of the broadcasting stations and not to any more fundamental set of principles; any deviation in practice from the principles the commissioners seek to uphold is left out account.

The previous chapter has provided ample evidence of the way the principles of the constitutions are ignored by the supervisory powers in the stations, and the insidious pressure on the broadcasters to conform to party-political patterns has been illustrated. There is nothing explicit in the constitutions to protect the broadcasters when the system is subverted. The various pressures on the system do curtail its freedom; they generate an internalized censorship – described here by Wolf Donner:

> ... it is less a question of concrete cases than of an atmosphere, of an indirect, difficult to prove, anonymous censorship. Programmes are stopped, re-worked, politically relativized, cut, postponed, placed in the archives; producers and their colleagues are put where they can do no harm, transferred, 'convinced' in discussions ...[5]

The pressure outside the stations pales into insignificance beside its internal manifestations in the area the political parties are attempting to dominate – and they are pursuing their objective most of the time within the bounds of the written constitutions. The broadcasters have attempted to counter this subversive infringement of broadcasting freedom by seeking institutional guarantees for themselves, or more precisely for their function.

The movement did not arise out of any theoretical or constitutional considerations, it was of a completely spontaneous origin.

During the period of the great CDU–SPD coalition (1965–69), opposition was almost non-existent in the *Bundestag*; people were made to think again about the meaning of parliamentary democracy, considerable political reorientation occurred and the interest of the parties in making their individual profiles known brought an increase in their activities in broadcasting. In February 1969, when student unrest – as students took over the role outside parliament of the opposition absent inside parliament – had already become a persistent and serious feature of public life, when more and more people were beginning to accuse the media of stirring up the situation, of generating conflict by their very presence at demonstrations, a demonstration at the *Land* Ministry of Education in Düsseldorf caught the officials completely off their guard – but was fully covered by a WDR television team. The reporters were accused not only of having prior knowledge, they were accused of setting up the whole incident. The idea was mooted that broadcasting journalists should be obliged to inform the authorities when they knew of impending action of a similar nature, thus bringing their status very close to that of state officials.[6] The idea was extremely farfetched, but it was discussed seriously in important circles both within and without broadcasting; in the eyes of the programme-makers it constituted a very real threat to their basic freedom of reporting. A spontaneous counter-reaction found support at all levels of WDR broadcasting personnel. The original suggestion was soon dropped, but the broadcasters had been warned, they had found new solidarity and felt the need to remain on their guard. Eventually they met for the first full assembly in the history of West German broadcasting of all the programme staff of one station (May 1969). The WDR intendant attended that meeting and seemed to welcome the step. It was decided to draw up a statute setting out the basic rights of the broadcasting staff.

The progress of the movement from the first assembly took the form of a bifurcation; while the movement of solidarity among the broadcasters spread eventually to all stations and all eventually drew up some form of statute, the discussions became fragmented as different bodies objected to different points. Progress was thwarted as basic issues were evaded, minutely detailed abstractions debated and subjects only remotely related to the original documents pushed into the foreground. In the end, although all the stations (with the exception of SWF) seem to have kept up the practice of the programme-makers' assembly, one station only emerged with a document called a statute. NDR has its 'statute for the programme-workers of NDR', the rest have arrangements in the form of directives and guidelines from the intendant or of modifications to the existing code of personnel representation.

The NDR arrangement is a weak one in terms of what the programme staff asked for, but it does refer to them specifically and it does recognize the existence and function of the assembly and of its committee within the framework of the station. The points conceded in the statute are granted to production staff as a group rather than to individuals, and they are granted outside the rights of personnel representation which apply equally to all employees, including broadcasting staff.

While the significance of the other arrangements must not be discounted, particularly intendant Wallenreiter's *Dienstanweisung* (directive) for BR staff and intendant Holzamer's *Leitordnung* (guiding rules) for ZDF staff, the NDR statute represents the best point of orientation for the consideration of the question of internal broadcasting freedom. It could prove to be an invaluable precedent for the future of the system.

A MEASURE OF SUCCESS?

The NDR statute can only be a point of orientation, it cannot be regarded in any way as typical. As conditions vary from station to station – often as a result of the differing constitutions – so also the statutes drawn up, the broadcasters' objectives, differed and still differ. The development of the movement in NDR does, however, reveal something of the general direction of events between 1969 and the present (1974). The statute alone does not fully meet the case as a point of orientation for the future; it must be seen in conjunction with the report which made it possible. This is the report by Dr Wolfgang Hoffmann-Riem,[7] which marked a turning-point in the evaluation of the broadcasters' demands and persuaded Schröder of the rightness of his course of action; it must now be seen as one of the major documents in the history of West German broadcasting. It is this work that could provide the basis at some later date for a reorientation in attitude to the broadcasters' demands generally; it offers an opening for a thoroughgoing examination of the essential nature of the freedom of broadcasting.

It is useful, before examining the NDR case more closely, to compare the course of events here with the very different pattern of developments in WDR, the point of origin of the movement; to a certain extent they represent the opposite extremes in the success of the movement. Both intendants showed an initial willingness to meet the programme staff, but whereas Schröder worked slowly towards a mutually acceptable solution, von Bismarck seems to have drawn back (it is not possible to say under what sort of pressure; his re-election was in the air while the end of Schröder's tenure of office was less imminent initially) until the document produced, the *Beteiligungsordnung* (arrangements for participation) offered his production staff hardly anything of what they had aimed for. They, quite rightly, view these concessions as minimal and have produced a document of maximal demands

(5 June 1972 – unpublished). This latter goes beyond anything they can hope to gain in the foreseeable future and represents a distillation of what the broadcasters feel they need by way of guarantees. This document, the fact that it exists, can be seen as a measure of the WDR broadcasters' disappointment at the reversal in attitudes to their position; it is certainly an indication of their determination not to be fobbed off for good with a genuflexion to outward appearances. Most groups of broadcasters, in fact, seem to view the present provisions as minimal, and all have some concept of a desirable maximum guarantee of their freedom; no other group has gone so far as the WDR group, no other group can feel so cheated.

The vital constitutional issues emerged most clearly in the NDR debate and can be educed from an examination of the evolution of the statute and a brief statement of some of Hoff-mann-Riem's main points.

The preamble to the original draft statute[8] (7 October 1969) opens with a full statement of article four of the NDR inter-*Land* agreement, which sets out the basic tenets for broadcasting in the station. The preamble then adds: 'The station is thus independent and neither subjected to, nor bound by group interests', and continues:

> The objective of this statute is to define more precisely the independence of reporting and the freedom to express opinion set down in article five, section one, sentence two of the Basic Law and in the inter-*Land* agreement, and to protect them from interference and attempts to exert pressure both from without and within. To this end, that is to secure the internal freedom of broadcasting, NDR – represented by the intendant – on the one hand, and the assembly of production staff (*Redakteursversammlung* – AW) – represented by the production staff committee (*Redakteursausschuss* – AW) – on the other, lay down the following principles ...

Thus, before any discussion and entirely of their own volition, the broadcasters endorsed the constitutional status of NDR and pledged themselves to join the intendant in establishing a number of principles to guarantee the fulfilment by the station of its constitutional obligations. There is not the slightest hint of an attempt to overthrow either the constitution or the intendant; the aim is clearly to resist the illicit pressures on the station by uniting the forces of broadcasting to uphold basic rights.

The main points the programme-workers wanted agreement on were very close to those embodied in the original WDR document[9] and included: the protection of the individual broadcaster against the overriding of his convictions (1); the securing of a flow of information and a right to express opinion on changes that would affect their work (changes in overall programme structure, in production structures, in individual contributions against the will of the contributor) – an explanation of such changes could be demanded by the full assembly of programme staff, who could turn to the public if the explanation given proved unacceptable (4); the right to express an opinion before senior appointments were made (5); the right to veto senior programme personnel changes, with this limited in the case of appointments to two candidates only, i.e. the veto was to provide a filter and a measure of protection against dismissals (6).

The final point in particular can only be understood against the background of party-political interference in appointments; it would have placed the intendant in an impossible position, for he would have been caught between the administrative council and the broadcasting staff. At best this point can be read as a warning that political interference in the appointment of senior programme staff had gone far enough; it was also a sign to the intendant that he would find support if he stood up to the administrative council. At worst it was a miscalculation by the statute-writers of the power of their position. The clause disappeared from subsequent versions of the statute – probably accounting for the progress it then made.

Intendant Schröder, who must have been subject to more pressure from the parties than any of his staff, was able to appreciate the underlying direction of the broadcasters' anxiety and showed considerable willingness to talk. The broadcasters themselves were not slow to respond. One can only conclude that there was a fair measure of goodwill, mutual respect and trust between the two parties.

On 2 July 1971 the full assembly of NDR programme staff approved a modified statute and offered it as a basis for negotiations[10] – they were already acting, *de facto* and with the consent of the intendant, as a separate group in the station. By this time they had seen that the fundamental principle at issue could easily be lost from view; the preamble was extended to clarify

THE FREEDOM OF BROADCASTING – AN INTERNAL PROBLEM

the concept of internal broadcasting freedom and to divorce it definitely from the field of labour relations and normal personnel representation:

> The internal freedom of broadcasting does not give grounds for any claim to co-determination in the general sense of labour legislation, but it does endow the individual programme-worker in the fulfilment of the journalistic tasks delegated to him in the sphere of information and opinion, i.e. of personal evaluating attitudes and commentary, with the legal power not to have to do or be responsible for anything that is contrary to his conviction.
>
> On the other hand, internal broadcasting freedom does not grant the individual programme-worker the right to disseminate his contribution from the station ...

but if his contribution is refused he has the right to know why.

The broadcasters were not concerned with wages and working conditions, they were not concerned with individual rights in general; they were concerned solely with the principles of their role as broadcasters, they were asserting their position, by defining it, in what had been a sort of no man's land similar to, indeed identical with, that occupied by the broadcasting service in society at large. They were beginning to see themselves as the embodiment of the vicarious function of broadcasting – even more so than the intendant who is a symbolic head, but not the performer of the actual function. They were beginning to say that broadcasting freedom matters most, perhaps matters only, where the actual programme is produced.

The designation 'programme-worker' was introduced for the first time in this document to make the relationship of the security demanded to the role (as opposed to the individual) incontestably clear, which in itself marked a step forward; a retrograde step was the omission from the document of a statement of the standing of the statute as an agreement between the station and the broadcasters, losing the valuable idea of consent. However, achieving the highest possible degree of consensus did remain a high priority in Schröder's actions and in the statutes movement in general. The broadcasters saw from the start that their claims could be binding only in so far as they were accepted as binding voluntarily by the intendant; they could never have been, they were never intended to be, enforced against his will. The attenuated veto the broadcasters claimed in this version (on the termination of contracts for reasons that infringe broadcasting freedom only) is further testimony to the fundamentally positive nature of their approach.

Following Hoffmann-Riem's submissions on the modified statute, Schröder set out to discuss the document widely within the station. Although the resulting alterations produced the rather bland final version of 31 October 1972, the intendant's intention was to gain the fullest approval for the statute to add to its internal standing. He acted in keeping with his understanding with the broadcasters and with the approval of the administrative council.

The statute eventually gained the approval of all parties in the station, including the personnel council and the trade unions, but not of the administrative council. It came into force on 15 July 1973 without its final article 12, which stated that it needed the approval of the administrative council. The most important body in the controlling structures of NDR dodged the issue of giving the statute (and hence the status of the programme staff) the crowning sanction by declaring it a matter not requiring its approval; it was deemed to be a matter for the intendant alone. The statute thus became an internal document with the status of a directive laid down by the intendant; legally it is no different from the steps taken in the other stations where the intendants issued directives without a prolonged discussion.

The content of the final document[11] is also much weakened; its preamble, for example, makes it a code for the resolution of conflicts. It defines the area the broadcasters were seeking to protect and sets some guarantees on the rights of the individual broadcaster, who cannot be forced to act against his convictions and who has the right to an explanation of changes made in his material. There is no veto of any kind. In the case of appointments and dismissals the broadcasters' representatives have only a right to be informed and heard; they can pass on their view to the individual directly affected and, in questions of basic principle, also expound it outside the station. They have no power of decision, their final court of appeal is the intendant and their only weapons are the deterrent of the explanation they can demand and the threat of turning to the public. If there was a hint in their first document that they saw themselves as a group with qualifications parallel to those of the broadcasting council, as a second legislature in the system on the side of public freedom, this has disappeared without trace in the final version. Their rights are secured in relation to the established structures of the station and it is stated expressly that they do not encroach upon the prerogatives of the controlling organs (clause ten):

1. This statute in no way detracts from the rights of the supervisory bodies and of the intendant.

2. This statute does not give grounds for co-determination as understood in labour legislation, in particular it does not detract from the rights of participation of the personnel council (*Betriebsrat* – AW).

No matter how pale a reflection of the original, the NDR statute does represent some positive gains. The broadcasters have clarified their own status, the term 'programme-worker' has been adopted. The right to meet as a body with a fixed status distinct from all others in the station and the right to work to maintain this position within the system through the committee have been accepted and chartered. In effect, the whole complex system of relationships within the station has been given new, more meaningful perspective by the definition of the concept of 'programme responsibility'.

Dr Hoffmann-Riem's analysis of the broadcasters' claims constitutes a further positive gain. Summarized very briefly (and inadequately) his case is that the internal structures of the broadcasting stations must enable the programme-workers to fulfil their constitutional duties. He submits that improvements in the existing system are necessary. The intendant's power of final decision is endorsed, but a case is also made for his power of delegation which construes this latter as including the right to delegate responsibilities to individuals and to groups within the station without reference to the administrative council; in meeting his constitutional obligations, the intendant can enlist the aid of his programme staff individually and in groups, as a whole if he wishes, and on his own authority. At no point is the question at issue that of employees' rights, this is a matter for the station's personnel council; the issue is always and only the proper performance of the broadcasting station's constitutional function.

Dr Hoffmann-Riem, however, does not confine himself to a constitutional and legal analysis, he adds a dimension of psychology and sociology to introduce the idea that changes of the kind outlined, which are possible within the existing legal framework, imply distinct advances in the management of broadcasting. By transforming a vertical hierarchy into a collegial system, cognitive stress (the pressure to conform to established views) is reduced and efficiency boosted. Conflicts are resolved by consultation and discussion underpinned by a free flow of information. In conjunction with his cogent legal arguments Hoffmann-Riem's management psychology, although not particularly original, rounded off a most convincing case.

All the statutes aimed at a greater flow of information and all the solutions achieved embody something of this principle. The BR intendant's directive amounted to an effort to introduce the collegial principle and the final NDR statute emphasizes the mechanisms for an increase in transparency and a sharing of responsibility. The modern management approach promotes a fuller, more open exchange between all levels of staff, breaking down the isolation of groups and individuals; above all it allows the top echelons of the station to identify with the programme-workers as they perform their common task. For the station as a whole the advantage proffered is greater cohesion and integrity.

In one important respect, however, Hoffmann-Riem's analysis has the same net effect as the administrative council's refusal to acknowledge the statute as more than an internal directive: the general situation his proposals encourage is one of integration into the establishment, rather than an overall readjustment of balance. Again the NDR solution can be seen as little different from the solutions found elsewhere.

The essential principle that Hoffmann-Riem propounds is the distinction between the individual and his function and, as a corollary, the demarcation of individual freedom from the freedom of the function, the freedom congeneric with the role. He uses the term *Freiräume* for the second concept – areas of activity where and for which a given freedom is granted. The activity itself is not possible without the freedom attaching to it and is the sole sphere in which that freedom is conceded.[12] The discussion of internal broadcasting freedom pivots on the recognition of this distinction as valid. The ability and authority to perform the function of public broadcasting are sanctioned in the concession of areas of responsibility and freedom, and the freedom of public broadcasting is guaranteed in the safeguarding of these areas. This concept marks the step forward in the theory of broadcasting freedom; it sets a new and vital point of orientation for the future.

THE GREATER DEBATE

In most stations the broadcasters' claims have been diffused in imprecise personnel arrangements;[13] similarly the clarity of Hoffmann-Riem's assessment was confounded by the weight of obfuscation that was generated in the wider debate. The main point of the broadcasters' movement and the crucial nexus of Hoffmann-Riem's case were studiously not addressed by the opponents of internal broadcasting freedom; the tendency was for the disputants to pick up points either at the periphery of the programme-workers' argument or from the most radical, unguarded utterances of the extreme left.

The opponents of the statutes movement seem to have concentrated their efforts on a few points only. They were preoccupied with the implications of the collegial system, which they attacked as unnecessary and as a negation of democracy. They denigrated the attempt to secure special protective rights for broadcasters as a move to gain extra elitist privileges. They claimed that the stations were not hierarchical, that delegation was the rule and not the exception. The collegial system, they said, was inefficient and obscured the issue of final democratic responsibility. Programme-makers, they thought, already had more rights than the intendant and to privilege them further would be contrary to the principles of pluralism and of equal rights for all workers.

A characteristic of the attack on the broadcasters was vagueness; loose usage was rife. The concept of the collegial system was distorted. The term 'co-determination' was used too often and imprecisely, as were 'internal broadcasting freedom' and 'democratization' (of broadcasting). The focus of attention was rarely the programme-workers and their situation; the whole question was always approached from the opposite angle, most commonly from the point of view of the intendant. If the opposition took account of what the programme-workers were saying and doing, they ignored the moderate developments and concentrated on a few loose comments from the early days of the movement, or from those areas where disaffection was greatest. It is true that all the commentators could claim that what they were attacking had been said or implied at some time by some representative(s) of the broadcasting staff of one or other of the stations; what they refused to see was the moderate attitude of the majority of the broadcasters – they failed to acknowledge the professionalism and serious-mindedness of most of the programme-workers with whom they claimed to work daily and whom they had appointed for the very qualities they were now seeking to deny them. The greater debate took on the form of the time-honoured German pastime, the *Literatenstreit*, where the emphasis is on the exercise, on the altercation, rarely on its subject and never on its solution.

As the statutes movement was construed by its opponents largely as an attack on the intendant, it is not surprising that the main opposition came from that quarter; in reviewing the ideas marshalled against the broadcasters we can limit our attention to the intendants, and in particular to the two who emerged as the strongest protagonists of the old order, Professor Bausch (SDR) and Dr Mai (SR).

Dr Mai has provided what, at the time of writing, seems to be the latest speech from the opposition – at the Institute for Broadcasting Law of Cologne University in mid-May 1974.[14] His first major contribution had been made some three years earlier and it is possible, by noting the changes in Dr Mai's awareness of the issues, to show how the focus of the debate has shifted since its inception.

In an interview reference[15] to his earlier speech, Mai differentiated unequivocally between the statutes movement and co-determination in a way that the broadcasters could only have endorsed:

Co-determination and production staff statute (are) two different things. With co-determination it is a question of whether members of the staff should have seats and perhaps votes in the supervisory bodies; with the statute the point at issue is the editorial freedom the individual producer can claim.

He went on to describe 'workers and staff' (*Belegschaft*) as 'not a socially relevant group'; the attempt to obtain representation for them was an attempt to make the agents under public supervision themselves the supervisors. Mai related internal broadcasting freedom to the freedom of opinion and set its limits where the pluralistic system of German broadcasting is infringed ... As long as the programme-maker moves within the area of this pluralistic journalistic responsibility, his activity will have no limitations imposed on it by me or by anyone else.

This point was repeated in 1974 and has been clung to by most commentators; their aim has been to set limits for the broadcasters, not to protect them from the actual pressures they are subjected to. The refusal to relate the problem to the practical situation resolved itself in the imputation to the programme-makers of designs on rights of co-determination, in the confusion of the two levels that Dr Mai was initially able so clearly to distinguish.

By 1974 Mai was beginning to relate the broadcasters' movement to the encroachment of the political parties on broadcasting freedom, but he did not see the one as a reaction to the other; he saw both as undermining the position of the intendant:

... Much more virulent (than the problem of the composition of the broadcasting council – AW) is the danger which, under the mask of the democratization of broadcasting and the so-called internal freedom of broadcasting, is at present threatening our democratic system of broadcasting, its supervision by their people and the mandated representatives, the broadcasting councils and the intendants. And the danger remains virulent which is threatening the freedom of broadcasting through the influence of the powers in the state and through other groups involved in government. Here occasionally unholy alliances are clearly distinguishable between programme-makers and political groups which really could endanger democratic broadcasting in the Federal Republic.

Dr Mai would clearly be right in his analysis, if his final sentence could be accepted at face value. However, he uses the link between the political influence on the system and the broadcasters' movement only as an argument to strengthen his case against the programme staff; it is posited by him to be what he wants it to be for the sake of his argument.

In the 1974 context his rejection of the statutes movement is part of a sophisticated descriptive analysis of the role and status of broadcasting in the state, which implies the imposition of strict limitations and obligations on the broadcasters. Broadcasting becomes, in Dr Mai's fascinating paper, a 'political quasi-authority' (*politische quasi-Gewalt*), a 'psychological indirect power of govern-

ment' (*psychologische mittelbare Herrschaftsmacht*). By analogy with
the state, the structures of control become transmission lines from
the citizens via the legislature (broadcasting council) to the
executive (intendant) which has a mandate from the people and
thus a right to issue directives to programme staff. This right is the
linchpin in the democratic system:

> The extension of the arm of the sovereign people through its repre-
> sentatives in the broadcasting council to the executive, the intendant,
> who is dependent on being elected and can be recalled, secures the
> retention of democracy in German broadcasting, and it is only
> possible on the basis of the right to issue instructions as described.

The argument for the transmission of control is irrefutable, if one
ignores the practical problems of ensuring proper public representation; the argument can be easily reversed to show that the
system in practice is the opposite of democratic. It is also clear
that groups within the stations must not be given the power to act
as representatives of the public in the sense of a second broadcasting legislature; it is not clear why they should have no protection against the intendant when the chain of command can be so
easily subverted. The protection of the broadcasters' function as
vicarious rather than mandated representation is not considered;
Dr Mai goes on to discuss the intendant's power of delegation and
reaches a point where his ideas are uncomfortably close to those
that started the original action among the programme-workers
in February 1969. He talks of confidence and trust, of loyalty comparable with that of civil servants and hints that the status of the
broadcaster is similar to that of the civil servant – except that the
intendant has no power to rid himself of disloyal staff comparable with that of the analogous head of a political office or
ministry. The suggestion he proceeds to make has since been
universally rejected:

> It ought to be discussed some time, whether the institution of the
> political official (*politischer Beamter* – AW) could not be introduced
> in some form into the personnel structures of broadcasting.

The appropriate point in the system would be at directorial level,
– in the senior appointments that the programme-workers were
wanting to redirect towards the programme and away from the
political forces in the system. Dr Mai's proposal amounts almost
to a cabinet system where the senior members of staff depend on

the intendant, probably sharing his mandate to some extent and all coming and going with him.

Such a change would be hardly significant in the context of Mai's own station where the intendant's unanimity with the supervisory bodies and with senior personnel in terms of political conviction could hardly be more pronounced. It is probably this background that explains why Dr Mai's main concern was that the intendant's position was weakest in the immediate area of programming where, in 1971, he had seen the intendant with less freedom than 'the individual colleagues who decide largely on themes and authors and edit the manuscript in question'.

Professor Bausch, an intendant in a situation similar to Dr Mai's, defended the intendant's authority to issue directives in September 1971[16] for exactly the same reasons:

I have to protest ... when the demand is made that no member of the production staff may be forced to admit or be responsible for a contribution to the programme which contradicts his own opinion (he uses the word 'opinion' and not 'conviction' – AW). The elected intendant can surely not be the only employee of a broadcasting station who for the sake of the pluralistic diversity of opinion is daily more or less forced to admit and be responsible for contributions which contradict his own opinion.

He also wants the whole team to act in accordance with the line taken by the intendant and seems totally to misconstrue the vital difference between the role of the intendant as an organ of the station with a supervisory and executive function and the role of the individual broadcasters. The former cannot in himself embody pluralism, he can only guarantee pluralism in the programme produced by the station, i.e. by a collection of individual broadcasters each of whom is permitted to make an individual contribution. The intendant must step in when pluralism is endangered, but not when his own opinion is contradicted; he must, by definition, permit views that are not his own. Conversely the individual programme-worker, whose name is associated directly with the content of the programme, must have the right to dissociate himself from opinion not his own. The refusal to include an item is not, as Bausch seems to imply, the same as the refusal to accept responsibility for it.

Professor Bausch, in fact, argues a case against co-determination which is seen as an infringement of the rights of the intendant and of the supervisory bodies. In summary, his views could almost be precursors of Dr Mai's 1974 ideas:

> A broadcasting station, where the staff determine 'democratically' who should be employed and who dismissed, where personnel representatives on the administrative council have the decisive say in the passing of the budget and where personnel representatives on the broadcasting council determine the outcome of the election of the intendant, is no longer an institution of mass communication which is independent of state and society and is controlled solely by the relevant groups in society.

Again the debate is carried away from the problems facing the system and nothing is gained by the overstatement ascribing the decisive voice to personnel representatives – especially when, in any case, the German could also be translated as 'tip the balance', a very necessary exercise in a public system whose balance is threatened by the bias towards the political parties and their minions.

Both intendants rely on theory and hypothesis for their arguments, and both tilt at windmills when neither would deny the need to add a dimension of democracy in the internal processes of the stations. Professor Bausch himself said:

> What one can demand with every justification is the internal 'democratization' of the process of decision-making within the station, the generous delegation of responsibilities, the activation of creative forces by a minimum of bureaucracy and a maximum of individual responsibility for colleagues.

It was a guarantee of this that the NDR broadcasters accepted and the BR and ZDF broadcasters were given, and that all broadcasters have in some shape or form since been granted.

Like Dr Mai, Professor Bausch was very close to the broadcasters at times, particularly in his early reactions, but again like his south German conservative colleague he allowed his eagerness to debate the subject in public to lead him away from them. Both intendants betray distinctly subjective traits in their stance and reasoning. A more objective view can be extrapolated from the comments of two other intendants of a quite different background, intendants Barsig and Bölling[17] from SFB and RB respectively. These saw the real threat to their position developing outside the stations; they reveal why the intendants felt that the system was being tampered with by strictly unconstitutional forces. Both are close to the SPD and both were provoked to make their comments by SPD policy statements.

On 6 November 1972 Barsig referred directly to the SPD paper on the media:

> In several places it says there that, in order to strengthen the journalists who make the programme, the intendant's right to issue instructions must be reduced and the hierarchical structures in the production sector replaced by collegial forms. In another place it talks about the democratic structuring of a station by a reorganization of the powers of decision and of responsibilities between the intendant and the staff. I say quite openly ... that I regard this resolution as having little practical relevance and in some points as unrealizable.[18]

He rejects the principles of organization suggested and, perhaps more strongly, rejects the attempts of bodies outside broadcasting to influence its structures. He describes the two dangers confronting the system: the increasing pressure from organized outside bodies (political parties) to influence the structure and functioning of broadcasting and, secondly, the change in broadcasting journalism towards tendentious reporting and mere opinion stating – he is very close to Hammerschmidt in his deprecation of this latter.

Bölling seems also to have seen political pressures as an expression of the same mood that produced the move for co-determination (the term seems justified in relation to RB) and the resistance of the broadcasters to the editing of (tendentious) work. In an article in *Die Zeit*[19] he is reported to have reacted to a local SPD suggestion that the collegial principle should be introduced (in radical form) in RB by stating that he was prepared to resign if it were implemented.

The two SPD intendants faced openly what their southern colleagues had only implied: the threat that held most potential danger for public broadcasting was a composite one. If the three areas in contention had been linked in a united front, the threat would indeed have been serious and the reactions to it understandable. If tendentious journalism were linked with the demand for more freedom and had the backing of a major political party, if the tendency in reporting were to the left, the move to eliminate or undermine authority of the left and the political support for

[155]

it from the left, then the fear of a great conspiracy would have been well-founded and would have met with more concrete support. The three areas do overlap: the SPD does support the idea of the collegial principle, the idea of greater co-determination – the *Jungsozialisten* even advocate the sort of takeover that Bölling was not prepared to tolerate; most obviously tendentious reporting is vaguely socialist, or at least anti-establishment, and the movement for broadcasters' rights has been led and kept alive by broadcasters with a strong left-wing tradition. However, the SPD did not have a monopoly of modern thinking on the management of the broadcasting media, the other parties endorsed the idea too; the development of the broadcasters' movement has shown that it was not a left-wing plot, the broadcasters have everywhere accepted what small concessions they could win and have continued to fulfil their public obligations; and the tendency towards committed reporting is, perhaps, less a sign of poor journalism than of journalists trying to find meaningful standards in a society slipping into complacent, self-fulfilling establishmentarianism. In the main, the three trends can be more easily and convincingly separated from each other than they can be conjured into some triple-strength chimera.

The programme-workers did not achieve their original objectives more than marginally, but they have won more than token recognition for their cause; they do not have institutionalized status as a body separate from all others in the stations, except in NDR, but in every station they have the right to speak as part of other representative bodies, and although their representation here is not always denoted as such, their identification as programme-workers has made their voice more distinct than it was previously. The significance of the movement derives as yet mainly from the debate, which has involved the broadcasters in the careful re-examination of their own status, has caused the intendants to think more constructively about their relationship to their fellow-workers and has placed the political parties in a position where they have had to talk seriously about broadcasting and look again at their own role in it. This general process of review and reassessment has, to date, produced no results of any moment, but it has come at a crucial time in the development of the West German broadcasting system when a major reappraisal as a foundation for the future seems inevitable. In any re-examination of the basic principles of public broadcasting in the Federal Republic, the points raised by the statutes movement will have to be considered; the movement will, perhaps, finally take its place in history, if the outcome of any deliberations marks the final break with the past, if actual pluralism and public control in broadcasting supersede the emphasis on written laws which screens the subversion of the system by the groups least qualified to participate in it.

CHAPTER TEN

More Public Broadcasting?

The late 1960s and early 1970s can be seen in retrospect as a period when the voice of the public in West German broadcasting, which had already in practice been pushed largely into the background, was in danger of being silenced altogether as crises both small and large broke upon the system. Most of these troubles seem now to be approaching a solution; the present period has the appearance of the lull after the storm. Out of it a constructive dialogue based on co-operation in the interest of the public service could emerge.

The events in Bavaria and the statutes movement are now sufficiently part of history for their real significance to become apparent. Both were an attempt to correct the perspective of the system when its pluralistic constitutional foundations seemed about to be undermined. In the Bavarian case the public acted to restore the pluralistic principle to its rightful dominant place; in the statutes movement the programme-workers sought to maintain a position that could have been lost, taking with it any real pluralism the system might hold – and they held their ground. Both actions were a response to the activities of the political parties; both administered something of a lesson to the forces of political life.

The CSU attempt to gain ground in Bavarian broadcasting also included a suggestion that private television should be admitted into the system. In this field the court ruling in Berlin and the first ruling in the Saarland[1] have, for the foreseeable future, virtually blocked any possibility of a break in the public monopoly. The public interest has been upheld here also.

The financial situation of broadcasting is rather different; here there is an urgent need for a major review. With the final decision in the ZDF taxation case the impulse necessary to bring all the relevant forces and factors together in a re-examination of the system could be given. The financial foundations of the system are not reliable; they do not offer a long-term guarantee of free and viable broadcasting, nor do they any longer provide sufficient security for the continued existence as independent entities of all the stations at present in operation to be assured. The solution of the taxation problem will involve a review of the licence system and of the weighting of commercial income; it will almost inevitably raise the issue of the smaller stations. A discussion of these factors could also be linked with a discussion of the *Land* boundaries and regional administrations. Since the latter complex of problems is also under review,[2] this in itself could initiate and will certainly add depth to a discussion of broadcasting structures – the chain of related questions would simply run in a different direction.

The discussion of these material problems could easily create an atmosphere in which questions of principle are overlooked. The positive events in the last few years, in Bavaria, in Berlin, and in the programme-makers' assemblies, have however provided a series of precedents and legal rulings which must underlie the consideration of any less fundamental issues. The way these questions have been resolved, perhaps more so than the actual results, offers a guide and a warning to the authorities who will be involved in the discussion of the material guarantees of the system. In Bavaria, in Berlin and in the broadcasters' assemblies the answers were found when one simple yardstick was applied – the public interest. The statutes movement wound down instead of becoming a confrontation and developing into a divisive crisis, because the programme-workers were prepared to accept compromises and small improvements; their action was never a threat to the public service, but will in time reveal itself as an additional service for the public, though not beyond the call of duty.

The problems as yet unresolved will be guided towards a positive solution if the people involved in tackling them are guided by this same yardstick; and these people are the ones who were rebuffed directly by the public in Bavaria and indirectly by the programme-makers: the *Land* authorities, the political forces in the *Länder*, and the political parties – the groups who, so far, have shown least respect for the public broadcasting service.

There are two small signs of a change in the attitudes of the party leaders. On the one hand, the discussions behind the scenes to find a generally acceptable political solution to the ZDF problem are promising to become a meaningful dialogue which could, because the existence of the system is threatened, progress beyond superficial considerations of political apportionment. If this should happen, then the general *ambience* could become conducive to progress in other areas. Secondly, the policy statements of the three major parties also hold out the possibility of change; if policy statements have any meaning at all, then there is some small sign that the lessons of the recent past have at least been noted for future reference.

PARTY POLICIES FOR THE BROADCASTING MEDIA

The three major parties have all published media papers and these can be used to assess what they think their attitudes to the media are likely to be in the future. The CDU group in the Hessen parliament and the *Junge Union* (Young Union, comparable with the Young Conservatives) have also published papers and there has even been a non-party paper.[3] The parties also publish the proceedings of their conferences, some of which include special working sessions on the media; all three parties now have media committees in one form or another. Yet another source of information on party-political and on less partisan thinking on the media are the regular conferences organized, in particular, by the churches and academic institutions.

The SPD paper agreed at the extraordinary party conference on 20 November 1971 was the first of the media papers. The CDU/CSU paper was offered to the public in April 1973 and the FDP completed the selection at the party conference held on 12–14 November 1973.

This latter paper is in many respects the least expected, bringing forward ideas that even the SPD did not spell out. Had intendants Barsig and Bölling[4] been members of the FDP they would no doubt have resigned their membership on the publication of this paper. It is tempting to suggest that only a small party with little chance of implementing its policies could formulate such radical ideas. The FDP proposals, if ever implemented, would entail a revolution in the organization of the broadcasting media. Because it is the latest and most interesting paper, the FDP contribution offers a useful point of departure for a brief examination of those parts of the parties' papers that are most relevant to the particular problems discussed above: the composition of the supervisory bodies, the roles of intendants and programme-workers and the relating of the broadcasting media to the public.

The discussion of the papers must be set against one important reservation: they do not indicate any change in the practice of the parties. The papers are couched in very sober terms, but passions still ride high when mention is made of co-determination and democratization in the context of broadcasting, as one brief example will show. The CDU/CSU media congress held in Munich on 30–31 May 1974 received a report from its 'Working Party II' (on broadcasting), which contains the following:

> The working party found far-reaching agreement in its view that the individual programme-worker's free expression of opinion is guaranteed within the framework set by the constitution and the laws. Assertions to the contrary are, therefore, to be taken primarily as the declaration of war of an ideological counter-movement, which defines broadcasting in our country, in deliberate misrepresentation of its pluralistic conception, as an instrument for the legitimation of monopoly capitalism and of the parties and associations that are its public support.
>
> This counter-movement, which takes its theses from neo-Marxist media theories, seeks as a first step on its way through the institution to replace the existing hierarchical structures with collective decision-making systems. This is called, disguised by a semantically questionable screen, 'democratization'.[5]

The FDP would hardly qualify as a neo-Marxist party and yet it is the party which emerges with the idea of replacing the intendant with a group of five directors, each with the supervision of one sector of the station's work and with one of them also assuming the chairmanship. The CDU sees the intendant as facilitating the supervisory function of the controlling bodies, but advocates development in the direction of modern management methods.

The SPD wants the intendant's right to issue directives to programme-workers curtailed and the workers given more co-responsibility.

The FDP directorate would be elected by the broadcasting council with representatives of the programme staff present and voting on the appointment of directors concerned in their areas of activity. These representatives would have the power to reject a candidate if they had the written backing of two-thirds of their representative body; this would be a part-veto which could be overridden by a vote of two-thirds of the appointing organ. These rights would be set out in a statute which would also contain guarantees that programme-workers would be kept fully informed and given a say in discussions prior to any decisions relevant to them and that their representatives would have the right on demand to put a case before the supervisory bodies. These guarantees are seen by the FDP as securing proper conditions for the fulfilment of the broadcasters' work; they would meet many of the requirements felt by the broadcasters themselves to be preconditions for the guarantee of their role.

The CDU/CSU and SPD papers do not suggest voting and partial veto rights for the programme-workers. The SPD advocates the participation of two representatives of the station's employees with voting rights in the administrative council and the CDU would restrict participation at this level to an advisory capacity, but both endorse the right to be heard and emphasize the importance of full information and dialogue. The idea of programme-workers' statutes and of representative assemblies is supported by FDP and SPD; the CDU does not oppose these ideas, it sees a use for programme-workers' committees and for the chartering of rights and duties in regulations for production staff (*Redakteursordnung*).

While it must be accepted that the papers are open to variations in interpretation in keeping with the nuances of formulation, there is nonetheless a surprising degree of agreement between them on two broad principles: modern management and written rights for programme-workers to meet as a group and to be informed and heard. It is also true that some of the differences in emphasis can be explained by the time-lag between the papers. The SPD paper was greatly influenced by the early stages of the statutes movement, the CDU/CSU and FDP papers by its later stages. The FDP paper came late enough to attempt an indication of the next stage in the development towards a reduction in the hierarchical structures of broadcasting.

A time-lag explanation seems also to relate to those parts of the papers which deal with the composition of the supervisory bodies. Here the Bavarian example appears to be the fulcrum.

The early SPD paper notes that broadcasting council meetings should be public. The CDU paper emphasizes that the work of the supervisory bodies must be given greater elucidatory publicity and that great care must be exercised in the (s)election of representatives to serve on them. The FDP wants public sittings of the supervisory bodies and also sets out a formula for membership which draws obviously on the Bavarian model. The three relevant paragraphs deserve full quotation:

> The broadcasting council comprises one-third of representatives of the parties in the respective parliaments and two-thirds of representatives of the socially relevant groups. It can elect additionally up to three qualified experts.
>
> Members of governments cannot be elected on to a broadcasting council; governments and administrations have no right of delegation.
>
> ...
>
> In the first third each party is to be given one basic mandate. For the rest the parties' representation is calculated according to the election result. The parties' representatives are to be elected by the parties at their respective party conferences.[6]

The socially relevant groups elect their own representatives at assemblies similar to party conferences.

There is some evidence that the SPD has moved in step with its partner in coalition towards the Bavarian model. In 1973, a report on a media conference held by the Protestant Conference for Communication (*Evangelische Konferenz für Kommunikation*)[7] says:

> SPD and FDP argued together for a reduction of party representatives in broadcasting supervisory bodies and thus for the introduction of the Bavarian broadcasting compromise in other *Land* broadcasting laws.[8]

Similarly the later CDU/CSU conference concerned itself with the composition of the supervisory bodies and noted the danger of state and parliamentary influence:

In view of the fact of the present, ascertainable predominance of representatives of executives and legislatures in some supervisory organs, and in view of the current practice of the political determination of licences by the parliaments, a certain danger lies ahead that this claim (to represent the whole of society – AW) will be infringed.[9]

Stress is laid on the selection of members and on a dynamic opening up of the supervisory bodies to representatives of the interested public, especially those organized in viewers' and listeners' action groups and the like.

The CDU parliamentary party in Hessen went further; it demanded a regular review of the relevance of the groups represented in relation to changes in society and also endorsed the Bavarian model.[10] The same point is made in the media paper of the *Junge Union*, which also calls for public meetings.[11]

Thus all the parties, at one level or another, endorse the idea of the proper investment of the broadcasting council with the qualities it is given in the written constitutions – with party, parliamentary and government representation together not exceeding one-third of the membership. Greater emphasis is also placed on direct representation for the societal groups and on the selection of people with relevant qualifications.

On the determination of licence fees and the removal of this process from complete dependence on the parliaments, the three also show a good measure of agreement. It is not clear from the CDU/CSU paper whether the call is for tighter control of finance or for more objective control – the paper refers to 'most stringent yardsticks' and leaves the decision to the parliaments; but the CDU/CSU conference did introduce the idea of objective mechanisms for the measurement of licence fees. The SPD advocated a federal commission to review licences, while the FDP suggested a committee of relevant experts to be convened at the request of the broadcasting authorities.

All three papers also agree on the need to ensure a greater supply of information to the public, and on the need to instruct and involve the public. Both CDU and FDP would encourage listeners' and viewers' associations, and the FDP would give them representation on the broadcasting council. The CDU/CSU paper and the Hessen CDU paper call for an effort within the education system to improve the public's knowledge and understanding of the media.

In mid 1974 the three parties seem closer to each other on these major points of broadcasting policy than at any other time; it is a position that has been reached in progressive stages over about three years. There must be, then, some grounds for believing that a general review of the system with all relevant groups involved could yield positive results in terms of a reaffirmation of public broadcasting; it could also bring a wider and more consistent implementation of the pluralistic principle.[12]

IMPLEMENTATION BY WHOM?

The parties may agree broadly on points that are of fundamental importance in terms of the democratic progress of the West German broadcasting system and this may even constitute a valid indication that important opinion is changing on these points towards consensus; but opinion, even consensus, is hardly a guarantee of change. Political parties have difficulty in implementing their policies when they are involved with one institution only; in the Federal Republic they have to work through 11 *Land* legislatures and in broadcasting through nearly as many institutions again – that is, if legislation and standing rules were the point at issue. In most respects the existing legislation needs no modification; what is necessary is a universal change of heart – first and foremost in the parties themselves. Here the credibility gap is enormous; party papers and the opinions of party spokesmen may say something about the attitudes of leading party members and even of delegates when they have to commit themselves in public, but they have little bearing on the behaviour and tactics of individuals and groups when they are involved in the realities of the struggle for political power.

It is in the nature of the parties and more particularly in the nature of the system that the various levels should fail to coincide. The whole is decentralized in its federal structures to the point where action is seen only in relation to individual parts. Each party-political attempt to gain influence in broadcasting seems, in itself, insignificant in terms of the whole system and yet, given the high degree of interdependence across the broadcasting services, interference with the balance at one point must have repercussions for the balance elsewhere. Meaningful change is only possible at a universal level, taking in all the stations from RB and SR through to WDR and ZDF. To bring all the various elements and levels into line – from the governments, through the parties to the societal groups, the public and the broadcasters – some generally applicable shock is required, a catalyst similar in effect but on a larger scale to the impulse that united the various forces in Bavaria.

The point at which something of this kind seems most likely to occur is in relation to NDR where the abuses seem greatest; but any change here would have to be endowed with universal and lasting significance for it to bring the requisite benefit to the system as a whole. The move that could achieve a result of this importance would be a confrontation of the parties, or of the NDR inter-*Land* agreement, with the law in the shape of the Constitutional Court. This sort of clash, effectively an uncompromising self-appraisal, could bring the principles set out in the media papers, which are in keeping with the pluralism of the constitution, to bear throughout the system.

The chances that the Constitutional Court will make a relevant ruling in the near future are real, and the threat to NDR does not come from within its own area, it comes significantly from the opposite corner of the Federal Republic.

The Constitutional Court has been asked to rule on the legality of the Saarland broadcasting law in so far as it admits the possibility of private broadcasting. The law allows the Saarland government to grant licences to private broadcasting companies; one such company, the *Freie Rundfunk AG* (Free Broadcasting Company) has attempted to establish in court that the law implies a right to a licence. Although the court ruled in principle that the law is not prescriptive but permissive, allowing the Saarland government to refuse a licence and, in the case in question, even to give no decision, doubt was expressed about the constitutionality of the clauses in the law governing the internal structures of any private company that might be granted a licence. Thus the case facing the Constitutional Court (a ruling was expected in 1975), although it seems on the face of it totally removed from the NDR situation, is about the internal structures of broadcasting and particularly the representation of the socially relevant groups. Since there is nothing to suggest that the court will modify the basic tenets of its earlier rulings, the public system with its institutionalized representation of the societal groups will almost certainly be endorsed again; and it is possible that the court will on this occasion devote closer scrutiny to the detailed composition of the supervisory bodies and make some clear recommendations on this. In so doing, it could establish a precedent strong enough for the simple threat of referral to the Constitutional Court to be sufficient to motivate the parties and the legislatures to review their roles in NDR and elsewhere. The Constitutional Court could, by its ruling, be instrumental in making all the various interests in broadcasting look critically and openly at the system in the light of the principles it is supposed to embody.

BROADCASTING AND THE PUBLIC

It would be wholly unsatisfactory and purely speculative to think in terms of a review of the broadcasting system solely on the basis of some future ruling of the Constitutional Court. And even if the ruling brings the result expected, it must remain ultimately only a court ruling. It is the task of the Constitutional Court to make the constitution live up to its words by speaking with all its authority for the spirit of the constitution; it can act to protect and, indirectly, to enliven the framework for the democracy the constitution would found, but democracy, to be meaningful, must exist outside written constitutions and legal pronouncements, it must exist in the minds of the people, in human relationships. All existing devices – constitutions, laws, court rulings, structures of control, management and participation arrangements – are only means to one end, the creation of a viable society, in broadcasting of a meaningful public service in the context of society, a meaningful relationship between the public and its broadcasting services. Democracy in broadcasting is, in the final analysis, a matter for the broadcasting authorities and their public.

There has been an increasing tendency for the broadcasting authorities to examine and improve their public relations, to find out more about the public and to tell the public more about themselves. This latter is important in the context of creating a unity of purpose about the maintenance and development of the service, but the importance of the former has also become increasingly apparent to the men in the stations. Here it is no longer a question of the weekly viewing figures and listening statistics, for there is an understandable scepticism in evidence now in respect of these as indicators of meaningful broadcasting. Increasingly the broadcasting authorities have turned to experts for scientifically based analyses of viewers' and listeners' habits and requirements, increasingly it is not the public's opinion as such that is considered but rather analyses of what type of person hears or sees what, when and where. The ZDF programme change in 1973, which entailed an earlier start to the main evening viewing, was based on an analysis of this kind and has been backed up in follow-up analyses to check the rightness of the decision. The radio 'service' programmes, the third television programmes, children's viewing habits, regional broadcasting requirements have all been the subject of similar examination. Hypothesis and the vicarious knowledge of the appropriateness of a programme for the public on the part of a few people who happen to be in senior positions in broadcasting are no longer the decisive factors in overall programming. These studies take some of the uncertainty out of broadcasting by giving the broadcasters a clearer objective and a more precisely defined public to serve; they inform the broadcasting authorities – but it is essentially a one-way process.

The stations have also become aware of a need and a duty to bridge the gap between themselves and their listeners and viewers. This aspect of their work is as yet only in an incipient stage, but already it has added a new dimension to their thinking; they are beginning to see the error of their earlier Olympian elitism and to modify their *ex cathedra* posture.

The real change came, to put an approximate date on it, about 1970. The need to inform the public about the financial situation had become apparent from the effort it had cost the broadcasting authorities to obtain the first licence increase (1 January 1970); this had been debated during the events of 1969 and the period of public disaffection when broadcasters had been seen as stokers of public unrest. This background, the events surrounding the re-election of von Bismarck, the incidence of controversial programmes (e.g. the NDR 'obscenity as social criticism' programme of 20 October 1970) put the stations under constant pressure to protect their image; they needed to redress the balance.

Preoccupation with an image, in itself, does not make for good broadcasting. Writing in 1970, Rainald Merkert pointed out that for broadcasting in a democracy the concern with image must not become more important than discussion and argument: 'the public must be respected as a partner to be taken seriously'; and in this context particular emphasis must be placed on the role of programmes about the media in the media. These are essential if broadcasting is to fulfil its function as the 'life-nerve' of democracy, the 'obstetrician of majority'.[13] The number of programmes about the broadcasting media has grown appreciably since 1970 and their quality is often excellent, but when Merkert was writing the attempt to find ways of cultivating an informed public was only beginning.

Almost a year later, Herbert Janssen was able to give the final section of an article on ZDF the title: 'Straitjacket for the programme, restrictive publicity policy'.[14] He noted that meetings of the ZDF supervisory bodies were not open to the public and found a parallel to this in the restricted flow of information within the station and in the embargo on the circulation of internal information outside the station. He proceeded to point out that ZDF had by that time established itself strongly as the rival of the ARD and, therefore, no longer needed to shrink from publicity:

> It can also be expected that both the station management and the programme-makers as well as the supervisory bodies will be more courageously frank than hitherto in the information about their work. And attention will also be paid within the station to a better flow of information, to more reasonable communication.

The next step seemed imminent; Janssen predicted that Professor Holzamer would use the occasion of his second re-election to sketch out a change of policy.

Change was, indeed, the theme of the address (17 February 1971) in which Holzamer saw 'television in the Federal Republic standing at a turning-point',[15] but the onus of his remarks was reserved for new methods of managing the station. He saw change in terms of the programme, but more so in relation to the broadcasters and their situation; he did not discuss information for the public. Klaus von Bismarck, speaking on 22 January 1971 after his re-election, also mentioned the requirements of the programme-workers; he did go on, however, to stress the need for information both within the station and in public. He admitted the inadequacy of the station's attitude to the public:

Public information about the situation of WDR is still inadequate in respect of important events, of changes in the programmes or productions and of the disclosure of the financial position.[16]

Although Professor Holzamer did not discuss public relations on the above occasion, ZDF did give considerable thought to this aspect of its work during 1971. For ZDF it entailed problems,

> which throughout the year became increasingly apparent and increasingly important: how could the relationship with the viewer be made more transparent and the viewer involved more in programme planning.[17]

The problem continued to haunt ZDF until in mid December 1973 the television council came to the conclusion that 'the station should seek to enlighten the public on the financial situation imposed on it by the taxation demands'.[18]

The need to be open with the public was universally apparent, particularly in relation to finance. ARD chairman-elect, intendant Hammerschmidt, for example, linked his first concern, the financing of the ARD (for which he wanted objective methods of assessment) with the public view of the broadcasting service. Hammerschmidt was certain of one thing:

> We have done too little with our own means to inform people about our work. And when we did, then it was with a limited aim and not always with unreserved openness. We will have to change this. The strongest denial is of less value than the facts which, if known, would make it unnecessary.[19]

Thus the stage seemed set for a campaign throughout the broadcasting system which would enable the broadcasting authorities to break down the barrier of ignorance that they themselves had created and which was now threatening to isolate them from the public altogether, reducing their security in both financial and political terms. Here, however, the disparateness of the system proved a weakness, and there was no action that could be termed a campaign. In fact, shortly before the ZDF television council decided to turn more to the public, intendant Hammerschmidt, then almost at the end of his period of office as ARD chairman (November 1973), complained that the public took broadcasting for granted – as much for granted as electric light. He had received letters of complaint about programmes often enough, but nothing on the serious and worrying developments facing the system.[20]

Hammerschmidt's successor as ARD chairman, Professor Bausch, echoed something of his predecessor's despondency in April 1974 in a paper he was to present to the ARD plenary assembly. *TV-Courier* reported on the relevant sections of the paper in the following way:

One of the next themes in the ARD chairman's paper: why does the popularity of the broadcasting system stand in an inverse relationship to the consumption of its products by the public? Professor Bausch holds the view that even the best information and explanation could never make broadcasting's specific expenses for radio and television fully comprehensible to broad strata of the population. No sort of 'transparency' could extend the limited judgement of wide sectors of the population ... 'There is no other public, or public law institution in this country which has to work so much in the shop window as broadcasting. What it does and lets be is observed with lynx eyes and commented on by specialist correspondents, programme magazines and the daily press. Its effective results can be checked by everybody in the programmes. Yet it is difficult for us to make the circumstances in which our production is carried out visible and, above all, comprehensible.'[21]

He was, however, still prepared to stress the need to inform the public 'in our own programmes'.

The remarks of the two most recent ARD chairmen share a certain confusion; neither succeeded in resolving the problem of informing the public. It is possible that, after two decades and a half of ignoring the public, the intendants experience the need to explain themselves as a sign of defeat, that they feel drawn out of their realm and exposed ignominiously. They fail to understand that the general public has the right to accept the broadcasting media as it accepts electric light, that they have no right to object because the majority of the public they serve will never understand the workings of broadcasting – it will never understand the production of electricity either.

The public is an audience which has the right to seek entertainment, to escape from information and education – and it will. In recent (1973) programme changes, this fact has been acknowledged without detriment to informational and educational programmes – the two activities are not mutually exclusive, they are complementary in that they aim at different publics. The intendants' remarks show that they have not respected their public sufficiently to get to know it properly; the work of enlightenment on matters relating to broadcasting must be aimed at a public that is already enlightened but not yet involved, the politically-aware public. This is a public that the broadcasting media can help to create and activate. Here Professor Bausch is unjust to the journalists who observe broadcasting professionally; they are as much guardians of the freedom of broadcasting as they are of the freedom of the press. He seems to forget the serious press which is strong in its support of the broadcasting system; whatever the degree of criticism, it is never designed to overthrow or cheapen the system. If the press is not solidly behind the broadcasting authorities and the public is not solidly behind them either, it is because the broadcasting authorities have not sought this kind of support until recently and they have not yet learned, they have not given themselves time to learn, how to ask for it, to win it and keep it.

The increase in the number of programmes about the broadcasting media, their work and their problems will improve the chances of a more open debate of these problems; and yet where specific difficulties are to be approached (finance, for example) even an enlightened public can only be a very indirect and tenuous link with the people who matter, the politicians who make the decisions. Here the broadcasting authorities must exploit the direct line of communication with these latter that exists already: the supervisory bodies. The intendants have failed to activate these as they have failed to activate the public. At an ARD conference on 13 December 1973, a perplexed chairman Hammerschmidt is reported to have said:

> Something happened in the main assembly which I have never seen in eight years' experience. The representatives of the supervisory bodies said quite clearly that their real task, that is, to be the link between the organizations in society (not only in parliaments) and broadcasting and to ensure the necessary level of information in the organizations they represent, has obviously not been fulfilled.[22]

The wheel has come round full circle. All the problems of broadcasting can be related to the one defective point in the system, the political element in the supervisory bodies. The line of communication between the public and the broadcasting authorities has one single flaw which affects the flow of information in both directions and blocks off broadcasting from the society that carries it.

BREAKING THE CIRCLE

Although the involvement of the public brings an improvement to the system, it has come too late to be significant in the present situation; perhaps it portends well for the future. Although the parties have set out some principles in their media papers that seem admirable, they have not shown any signs that they intend, or even know how to start implementing them. The Constitutional Court could provide the impetus needed to bring improvements to the system, but more necessary than this is an effort on the part of those involved in broadcasting to keep reminding the parties of their words and of their failure to act. The stations have the right, the duty and now also the policy to keep the public informed, to keep the issue alive through their programmes and through general publicity work. They have the obligation to exert pressure on the representatives of society in their own supervisory bodies to become two-way channels, to undo the errors of the past and secure a more mature future.

In the attempt to reorient the system pressure can be applied in relevant quarters on specific issues and also on questions of more general principle. Professor Bausch, in the paper referred to above, linked the two levels in a challenge to the political arbiters of the system:

> If the broadcasting stations are to continue to work meaningfully, then the question must be put and answered, what relative value in society is to be granted to broadcasting and what it may cost.[23]

It is, perhaps, wrong to link the question of finance with a point of such fundamental importance. The question of the role and value of broadcasting is being asked and answered all the time. If it is in any way a question of finance, then it is this only peripherally. The price of freedom in broadcasting is not measured in monetary terms, as Sir Hugh Carleton Greene said in a German television programme in 1971:

> The price of freedom is constant watchfulness and resistance to pressure. Show me a country in which broadcasters and politicians

are often at odds, and I shall show you a society which is freer than most.[24]

There could be no better time than the present for broadcasting people in the Federal Republic to launch an offensive to secure the freedom of broadcasting; the question about the relative value of broadcasting will have to be answered in the near future, perhaps more clearly than it has in the past, by both politicians and public. Now, however, there is no great battle to be fought to preserve broadcasting as a public responsibility in the face of government and commercial interests; now the problem is to come to terms with what already exists, to decide on this basis what the role of broadcasting is to be for the future. The West Germans have a public broadcasting system which is founded in law and buttressed about by the rulings of the Federal Constitutional Court, but in it they also have a system in which the pluralistic ideal has been subverted and submerged; the service has never been finally and irrevocably turned over to the public. The system has, so far, progressed by a series of steps, each of which has brought something to strengthen the public interest. The past five years have, perhaps, been the darkest for the public's voice in broadcasting, but they could yet prove to be the foundation for a more significant step forward than any so far in the system's history. The past few years have seen something of an awakening of the public's interest in broadcasting and of broadcasting's interest in the public.

Professor Bausch was asking whether the step forward would come, or whether the system will be allowed to stagnate and atrophy. He will not get his answer from the public – the process of enlightenment has not yet proceeded far enough; he might get an answer of sorts from the political forces in the state – but it will be an answer to the question as they understand it. His answer, the answer he wants and the answer society deserves, can be given only by those to whom society has entrusted its public broadcasting system already, by those who fully comprehend the point of the question: the broadcasters and, above all, the intendants.

The intendants can demonstrably resist the pressure of the parties; they can speak for the system to the public both directly and through the linking bodies, and they alone can lead the broadcasters in their work and protect their freedom at their work. The

[174]

opportunity is given: the programme-workers have shown their willingness to co-operate in the interests of the system, the public has demonstrated that it will not tolerate open manipulation of the system, the political parties have hinted that the warning to them has been heard in some quarters that matter, and the prime ministers of the *Länder* are already actively discussing the most difficult financial problems. The situation cries out for positive leadership; it leaves no room for perplexity or apathy, nor for hasty and overstated challenges. The time calls for a critical review of the system by the broadcasting authorities themselves and for leadership from them. The intendants are in the unique position of bestraddling the gap between the two sides of the system, the public control and the public service; this is their appointed task, their vocation in society. They must debate and answer the question among themselves and with the two pillars of the system, the members of the supervisory bodies and the programme-workers. Above all else, they must debate and define their own position anew to prepare themselves to cope with a situation of imminent change.

Self-criticism and reappraisal are essential in a transitional phase, and in broadcasting in West Germany the mid 1970s are surely this. The intendants must take stock of the system that they and their predecessors have created, they must evaluate the changes that have taken place as a result of the influence of their system on society and they must assess how they can best prepare themselves and the system for a role in the mature West German state. In this way broadcasting will remain a vital factor in the process of bringing the meaning of democracy in Germany to a new level. The words of Hans-Geert Falkenberg could be repeated in this context – substituting broadcasting for television and seeing broadcasting in the symbolic figure of the intendant:

> ... but I'll risk the thesis, that only the criticism of television through television itself will liberate the viewer from his minorship, and that the end of one monopoly consciousness will not be made manifest in the establishment of new, more dangerous monopolies, but only in a viewer who has been given his majority and given sight, who has been emancipated.[25]

The education of the public to democracy is in a crucial stage in the Federal Republic. West German society has at last reached the

point where it seems to have put the past finally behind it; it has at
last embarked on its own history as a state which will not be
united with another Germany, as a state with fixed political, constitutional and geographical boundaries. Internally the need for
the public to hide behind powerful, unchanging leaders is past;
effective parliamentary democracy could be brought a step closer
to realization. The public has shown on several important occasions that it will have its say, and that when it does it has a clear
voice for democratic principles. The leaders of industry and of the
economy have shown that they have the confidence in themselves,
in their economic strength and in the good sense of their workers
to allow almost universal rights of co-determination. The same
confidence is not yet apparent in the political forces in the state
in their relationship with the public; there is still apparent here
something of the old 'super- and subordinate' attitude – and
nowhere more so than in their dealings with the broadcasting
media. Here the evils of the two-party system have been made
blatantly obvious; two-party democracy is hardly parliamentary
democracy, and is certainly not meaningful pluralism. The artificial
state of confrontation which so easily becomes established under
these conditions is the negation of democracy; it is neither a reflection of the public mind nor an effective vehicle for progress. The
solution to the self-imposed deadlock that is increasingly undermining western democracies is an effective public voice immune
to the same ossification.

In the Federal Republic the intendants can still assert the voice
of broadcasting, the voice of the public. They have been given a
breathing space by the acceptance on the part of the programme-
workers of the statutory concessions made to them; the way to
fruitful teamwork is still open. The parties have offered them a
chance to save themselves from the grip of frozen confrontation.
They have not abandoned their task of talking with and informing
the public. The changes brought about by the problems of the
1960s and early 1970s have placed the heads of broadcasting in a
new position with new responsibilities in relation to society; they
are no longer the executive heads of mere broadcasting stations,
they are the managers of modern, enfranchised democracy. Their
awareness of their role in the present situation will determine the
course of West German broadcasting, perhaps also of the West
German democratic system.

The intendants must rise above the fears and suspicions generated by the system, above the dissension, stringency and uncharitableness that characterize public life. They must strive to attain to the stature demanded of them by their role in society; they must be guided solely and unswervingly by their unique duty to serve the public in broadcasting.

Notes

INTRODUCTION

1. FK, 14/70, 2.iv.70, 2.
2. MP, 11/73, 538.

CHAPTER ONE

1. Translated from the German. Siegler, 64.
2. From the English version.
3. Ditto.
4. NWDR was founded by the very brief Military Regulation No. 118.
   The text referred to is in the accompanying standing rules. Brack,
   133–143 (here, 135); Fischer, 98.

CHAPTER TWO

1. Translated from the German. Fischer, 102–103.
2. Hood, 13. Hood uses the term 'federation' in the text.

3. An excellent article in the *ARD Jahrbuch 1969* (19–49) by Rainulf Schmücker: 'Unabhängigkeit und Einheit. Wie die ARD entstanden ist', describes Bredow's role in full and gives a more complete picture of the events leading up to the founding of the ARD. Fischer also contains documents relevant to Bredow's work in both of his periods of active involvement in broadcasting (here, particularly 89–90) and a useful chronicle of events in broadcasting (37–46, in particular).
4. ARD, 54–56; Brack, 127–132; Lehr, 261–264.
5. Left in the original to avoid the possible misinterpretation of translations used elsewhere as anything more than helpful suggestions.
6. Cf. Fischer, 104–109.
7. Ibid., 115–117.
8. Ibid., 120–126.
9. Ibid., 132–147.
10. Ibid., 158–162.
11. The *Spiegel* affair is the subject of thorough documentation and analysis in two volumes edited by Jürgen Seifert.
12. Quoted by Flottau, 53.
13. Cf. Flottau (53–59) for an account of events at this time; also Lilge, 99–102.
14. Fuhr, 228–259; Lehr, 221–256.
15. Lehr, 234.
16. Loc. cit.
17. Ibid., 235.
18. Ibid., 236.
19. Ibid., 221.
20. Ibid., 245–246.
21. Ibid., 255–256.
22. Ibid., 256.
23. Ibid., 255.
24. The translation here is literal, the point is crucial in the reading of the ruling.
25. Loc. cit.
26. Ibid., 254.
27. Ibid., 161–170; Brack, 185–200; Fuhr, 15–28.

CHAPTER THREE

1. Useful short articles on RIAS, DW and DLF can be found in the ARD yearbooks as follows: 1971 (44–49), Roland Müllerberg: 'Für Berlin und Deutschland. Der RIAS – Rundfunk im amerikanischen Sektor'; 1969 (103–106), Walter Steigner: 'Für Hörer in aller Welt. Die Deutsche Welle'; 1970 (58–63), Franz Thedieck:

'Für ganz Deutschland und Europa. Der Deutschlandfunk'.

2. Calculated on the basis of statistics published annually in the ARD yearbooks.
3. ARD (69–80) offers a set of interesting and relevant maps.
4. Ibid., 9.
5. In the revised version (1964) in ARD (39–41) and Lehr (283–286).
6. ARD, 37–38.
7. See 5 above.
8. ARD, 12.
9. A useful short article on the *Telekolleg* can be found in *ARD Jahrbuch 1969*, 172–174 (Helmut Oeller: 'Weiterbildung für jedermann. Das Telekolleg'). Flottau (100–103) also provides some interesting information.
10. ARD, 44–45; Lehr, 296–297.
11. TVC (20/74, 17.vi.74, 10) offers some relevant statistics. In the combined SR/SDR/SWF (*Südwest 3*) *Telekolleg I* (1969–71) there were 11,152 participants of whom 33 per cent gained certificates; in 1974 (1971–74) 51 per cent of 3,294 registered students were successful. In the *Telekolleg II* (1972–74) about 39 per cent of 3,504 participants were expected to sit and pass the examinations. In the same geographical area, the radio courses had (by 1974) registered some 130,000 students (52 per cent teachers), of whom some 25,000 had been awarded certificates. These are two examples only of the type of course available.
12. ZDF inter-*Land* agreement §22(4) and the introductory paragraph to the temporary agreement between the ARD and ZDF of 18 September 1967 (ARD, 46).
13. ARD, 46–47. For the co-ordination agreement of 19 May 1972, see *ARD Jahrbuch 1972*, 287–288. A new 2-year agreement, designed particularly to improve the balance of weekend programmes, came into force in January 1976.
14. ARD, 42–43; Lehr, 292–294.

CHAPTER FOUR

1. For the former: *ARD Jahrbuch 1969*, 319–321; Lehr, 256–259. For the latter: *ARD Jahrbuch 1971*, 238–250; Fuhr, 260–283.
2. *ARD Jahrbuch 1970*, 297–302; Fuhr, 223–227; Lehr, 23–27.
3. TVCD, 17/74, 13.v.74, 1.
4. MP, 3/73, 124–126.
5. Lehr (32–42) has a summary of the regulations for exemption.
6. *ARD Jahrbuch 1972*, 232.
7. ARD, 50–53.
8. MP, 4/74, 174–177.

9. Calculations from statistics in the respective yearbooks. The term ARD is used very loosely here; the ARD as such does not have a net income.

10. Flottau is strong on this aspect of German broadcasting (226–233).

11. MP, 6/73, 284. MP is an invaluable source for statistics of this kind.

12. ARD, 48–49.

13. Ibid., 12.

14. The figures are taken from very disparate sources and should be regarded as no more than the barest indication of what is involved.

15. MP (6/74, 290) shows for April 1974 the expenditure on advertisement in the press (as a whole) as DM387,301,000, for radio as DM28,079,000 and for television DM83,828,000.

16. Ernst W. Fuhr: 'Werbeeinnahmen des ZDF steuerpflichtig?' (*ZDF Jahrbuch 1972*, 115–123).

17. Ibid., 122–123.

18. Figures approximate. Cf. TVCD, 1/73, 8.i.73, 10; the ZDF *Finanzvorschau. Voraussichtliche Haushaltsentwicklung in den Geschäftsjahren 1973 bis 1979*, 22–23 (ZDF document of late 1972); the annual financial reports in the ZDF yearbooks (e.g. 1973, 135) also refer regularly to this situation.

19. The translation is literal; the simple present tense in the German is the source of many of the station's problems.

20. *ZDF Jahrbuch 1962/64*, 17.

21. Cf. TVC, 42/73, 10.xii.73, 3–8 and I-VI; TVC, 20/74, 17.vi.74, 6.

22. Basic Law, articles 105–107.

23. ZDF: *Finanzvorschau. Voraussichtliche Haushaltsentwicklung in den Geschäftsjahren 1973 bis 1979*, 21.

CHAPTER FIVE

1. *ARD Jahrbuch 1971*, 238–250; Fuhr, 260–283.

2. KR, 38/74, 29.v.74, 1–2 and I-II; cf. also MP, 9/72, 421–428.

3. Cf. 166 for a comment on the significance of this case.

4. *ARD Jahrbuch 1972*, 295–304.

5. Cf. 25–26 on the founding of the company.

6. *ARD Jahrbuch 1969*, 319–321; Lehr, 256–259.

7. *ARD Jahrbuch 1972* (280–286) contains a projection for the years 1972–75 (*Zahlenwerk II*) and discusses the relation of losses from licence exemptions to potential increases in licence income (281). In the later, revised version (published by the ARD, December 1972) the figures (13–14) show a worsening situation. Cf. Table 1 for an indication of the proportion of free licences; some predictions suggest that ultimately 8 per cent of all licence-holders will

be given exemption. Additional licence exemptions in the period 1973–75 were expected to deprive the stations of DM100m.

8. The quotations are not from the ruling itself but from a press release and a summary of the ruling contained in TVCA, 41/71, 17.viii.71, 1–14; here, 2 (Fuhr, 278).
9. Ibid., 1 (Fuhr, 268).
10. Ibid., 6 (Fuhr, 267).
11. Ibid., 11 (Fuhr, 174).

CHAPTER SIX

1. Herbert Janssen in an article based on the transcript of a WDR radio discussion. FK, 19/71, 6.v.71, 4.
2. Gerhard Wahrig: *Deutsches Wörterbuch* (Gütersloh, 1973).
3. Lehr, 255.
4. There were two commissions in the late sixties headed by Dr Elmar Michel. The first reported on the 'equality of competition between the press, radio/television and film' to the federal government in 1968. The second started work later in the same year on the 'development of broadcasting in the south-west area' – an investigation undertaken on behalf of the *Länder*: Baden-Württemberg, Rhineland-Palatinate, Saarland. Its report was completed in early 1970 and printed as such but, sadly, never published in book form. The references here are all to the second commission.
5. Michel, 7.IV.H, 203–4.
6. 6/71, 1.ii.71, 43–45.
7. TVCAD, 51/72, 27.xi.72, 6.
8. TVCD, 26–27/74, 15.vii.74, 19.
9. *Der Spiegel* (44/72, 23.x.72, 75–89) has a full and not very complimentary article on *ZDF-Magazin*.
10. For example, at a press conference in Baden-Baden on 15 May 1974. KR, 36/74, 18.v.74, 4–5.
11. RF, Vol. 19 (1971) (178–188) has these two and two intermediary documents.
12. Ibid., 187.
13. Ibid., 184.
14. Cf. *Der Spiegel*, 5/72, 24.i.72, 51; and 6/72, 31.i.72, 119–120.
15. TVC, 16/74, 20.v.74, 5–8.
16. TVC, 11–12/74, 8.iv.74, 1 and 7–8.
17. TVCD, 12/74, 8.iv.74, 7c–7d.
18. TVC, 11–12/74, 8.iv.74, 8.
19. Michel, 10.IV, 271.
20. TVC, 11–12/74, 8.iv.74, 3–4; TVCD, 12/74, 8.iv.74, 7a.

CHAPTER SEVEN

1. Michel, 198–199.
2. Ibid., 201.
3. Ibid., 202–203.
4. Lehr, 57–63 (standing rules, 63–68).
5. Pursuant to the Hessen law on personnel representation, 14 February 1970.
6. Lehr, 126–132 (standing rules, 132–146).
7. Cf. 91.
8. There are also in SWF advisory members who can be co-opted (since 1952) for their special expertise. They do not represent any particular societal or political group.
9. Lehr, 146–153 (standing rules, 153–160).
10. Ibid., 68–76 (standing rules, 77–85).
11. 16 February 1955 and 25 May 1954.
12. Military Regulation No. 118. Brack, 133–143.
13. In particular ZDF, but also SR, DW and DLF. Cf. 20–27.
14. Cf. 131–133 for the importance of this lacuna.
15. The Bavarian constitution permits the process practised here, whereby the people can request (*Volksbegehren*) that a point of law, particularly a change in the constitution, be referred to the people for its approval (*Volksentscheid*).
16. Lehr, 45–53 (standing rules, 54–56).
17. Text kindly supplied by BR.
18. MP, 3/72, 141–142.
19. MP, 4/72, 192.
20. MP, 11/72, 513.
21. Text kindly supplied by BR.
22. MP, 5/73, 228.

CHAPTER EIGHT

1. The choice of examples has been kept to a minimum and, where possible, to sources that can be available to the reader.
2. FK, 27/70, 2.vii.70, 8a.
3. FK, 28/70, 9.vii.70, 1–2a.
4. The ARD yearbooks contain details of the membership of the various supervisory bodies.
5. *Der Spiegel*, 41/71, 4.x.71, 97.
6. *Medium*, November 1973, 3.
7. Manfred Jenke: 'Alle Macht den (Rundfunk–) Räten?', *Der Monat*, Vol. 23, No. 270, March 1971, 42.

8. Described by Herbert Janssen in FK, 7/71, 11.ii.71, 5a.
9. Reported in KF, 18/72, 13.v.72, 5–7.
10. TVC, 15/71, 19.iv.71, 6.
11. *Medium*, November 1973, 3 and 13.
12. KR, 36/74, 18.v.74, 2–3 and 38/74, 29.v.74, 9.
13. KF, 12/72, 25.iii.72, 1–2a.
14. KF, 15/72, 22.iv.72, 8–9.
15. *ARD Jahrbuch 1972*, 188.
16. Herbert Janssen; FK, 48/70, 26.xi.70, 3.
17. FK, 14/71, 1.iv.71, 5–6.
18. 45/73, 5.xi.73, 207.
19. This becomes apparent from events reported in FK, 39/73, 26.ix.73, 1–7 (particularly 3).
20. TVCD, 2/74, 15.i.74, 10.
21. *Die Zeit*, 8/74, 15.ii.74, 5.
22. From the German. In a part transcript of 'Glashaus – TV intern' (WDR, 23 December 1973); TVCD, 2/74, 15.i.74, 14.
23. TVCD, 48/73, 10.xii.73, 5.
24. (a) 30/71, 19. vii.71, 58; (b) 39/71, 20.ix.71, 195; (c) 29/72, 10.vii.72, 52.
25. 41/71, 82.
26. *ARD Jahrbuch 1972*, 12.
27. *Süddeutsche Zeitung*, 7.v.73.
28. 38/73, 14.ix.73, 17.

CHAPTER NINE

1. The trade union of the mass communication industry. Cf. Helmuth Haselmayr: 'Eine Gewerkschaft für Rundfunkleute. Die Rundfunk-Fernsehen-Film-Union im DGB', *ARD Jahrbuch 1972*, 17–23.
2. KR, 36/74, 18.v.74, 1.
3. Miss Richards (see acknowledgements) has devoted her personal research effort to a full analysis of the implications of the broadcasters' movement from the point of view of the production situation as a set of circumstances which inhibit democracy in practice. It is hoped that her dissertation will be available soon in the University Library, Bradford.
4. Michel, 7.IV.G.3, 203.
5. *Die Zeit*, 11/71, 12.iii.71, 19.
6. Basic Law, article 35: 'All Federal and *Land* authorities render each other mutual legal and administrative aid'.
7. Published by Nomos Verlagsgesellschaft, Baden-Baden, in 1972 as *Redaktionsstatute im Rundfunk*.

8. This and a few other early documents are published in Skriver 129ff.
9. Cf. Alexander von Cube: 'Zögernde Emanzipation. Zu den Redaktions-Statuten', *Der Monat*, Vol. 23, No. 270, March 1971, 45–50.
10. Text in Hoffmann-Riem, 195–197, and FK, 28/71, 8.vii.71, 10–12.
11. RF, 2–3/21 (1973), 261–263 (with notes, 263–266).
12. Hoffmann-Riem, 92–96.
13. The new federal law on personnel representation (15 May 1974) will promote this process.
14. TVCD, 19/74, 27.v.74, 8–17.
15. TVC, 44/71, 29.xi.71, 3–9.
16. TVCAD, 3.x.72, 1–4.
17. Bölling has now become *Regierungssprecher*, Head of the Press and Information Office of the Federal Government with the equivalent rank to Permanent Under-Secretary (20 May 1974).
18. TVCAD, 13.xi.72, 12.
19. 43/73, 19.x.73, 18.

CHAPTER TEN

1. Cf. 67.
2. It is uncertain whether any changes will result; a series of referenda on the question is expected in late 1975.
3. Issued by a group representing business interests. TVC, 42/72, 4.xii.72, 3–7.
4. Cf. 154–156.
5. MP, 6/74, 270.
6. MP, 11/73, 542.
7. 2–3 April 1973 at the Arnoldshain Academy.
8. MP, 4/73, 168.
9. MP, 6/74, 269.
10. TVCD, 19/74, 27.v.74, 2.
11. Ibid., 1.
12. MP is an excellent source for the media papers: 6/73 (265–278) contains the CDU/CSU paper, 7/73 (334–343) has a contrastive synopsis of the three papers and 11/73 (538–547) gives the FDP paper in full. TVCAD, 27.ix.71, 1–6, contains the draft SPD paper.
13. FK, 14/70, 2.iv.70, 1–4.
14. FK, 7/71, 11.ii.71, 5a-5b.
15. TVCAD, 1.iii.71, 1–3.
16. Ibid., 6 (full speech, 4–6).
17. *ZDF Jahrbuch 1971* (11) with reference to the annual 'Mainzer Tage der Fernseh-Kritik'. Each of these annual conferences gives

rise to an excellent volume in the series *Fernseh-Kritik,* published annually by von Hase und Koehler Verlag, Mainz.

18. TVC, 43–44/73, 17.xii.73, 7.
19. TVCAD, 6.xii.71, 3.
20. TVCD, 48/73, 10.xii.73, 1–2.
21. TVC, 14/74, 29.iv.74, 2a.
22. TVC, 43–44/73, 17.xii.73, 5.
23. TVC, 14/74, 29.iv.74, 2a.
24. From the German. TVCAD, 1.xi.71, 2.
25. TVCAD, 26.x.71, 12.

Bibliography

PERIODICALS (SPECIALIST)

FUNK-Korrespondenz. Katholisches Institut für Medienforschung
e.V., Cologne.

Kirche und Fernsehen. Now *Kirche und Rundfunk.* Gemeinschaftswerk
der Evangelischen Publizistik e.V., Frankfurt-am-Main.

Media Perspektiven. Arbeitsgemeinschaft Rundfunkwerbung,
Frankfurt-am-Main.

Medium. Evangelische Konferenz für Kommunikation, Frankfurt-
am-Main.

Rundfunk und Fernsehen. Hans-Bredow-Institut für Rundfunk und
Fernsehen an der Universität Hamburg.

TVC-Archiv and *TVC-Archiv/Dokumentation.* Now *TV-Courier*
and *TV-Courier/Dokumentation.* TV-Courier Verlagsgesellschaft
mbH, Wiesbaden-Bierstadt.

PERIODICALS (NON-SPECIALIST)

Der Monat. No longer published.
Der Spiegel. Hamburg.
Die Zeit. Hamburg.
Süddeutsche Zeitung. Munich.

COLLECTIONS OF DOCUMENTS RELEVANT TO BROADCASTING

BRACK, HANS, HERRMANN, GUNTER and HILLIG, HANS-PETER. *Die Organisation des Rundfunks in der Bundesrepublik Deutschland 1948-1962.* Hamburg, 1962.

FISCHER, E. KURT. *Dokumente zur Geschichte des deutschen Rundfunks und Fernsehens.* Göttingen, 1957.

LEHR, WOLFGANG and BERG, KLAUS. *Rundfunk und Presse in Deutschland.* Mainz 1971.

INDIVIDUAL WORKS RELEVANT TO BROADCASTING

Arbeitsgemeinschaft der öffentlich-rechtlichen Rundfunkanstalten der Bundesrepublik Deutschland: *Denkschrift über die Zusammenarbeit der deutschen Rundfunkanstalten.* December 1967.

FLOTTAU, HEIKO. *Hörfunk und Fernsehen heute.* Munich 1972.

FUHR, ERNST W. *ZDF-Staatsvertrag.* Mainz 1972.

HOFFMANN-RIEM, WOLFGANG. *Redaktionsstatute im Rundfunk.* Baden-Baden 1972.

Bericht der Kommission zur Untersuchung der rundfunkpolitischen Entwicklung im südwestdeutschen Raum. Second Michel Commission, 19 January 1970 – unpublished.

SKRIVER, ANSGAR. *Schreiben und schreiben lassen.* Karlsruhe 1970.

ANNUAL PUBLICATIONS

ARD Jahrbuch 1969 (ff.).
ZDF Jahrbuch 1962/64 (ff.).

OTHER WORKS REFERRED TO IN THE TEXT

Grundgesetz für die Bundesrepublik Deutschland.
The Basic Law of the Federal Republic of Germany. Prepared by the German Information Center, New York.

HOOD, STUART. *The Mass Media.* London. 1972.

LILGE, HERBERT. *Deutschland von 1955-1963.* Hanover. 1965.

SEIFERT, JURGEN. *Die Spiegel-Affäre.* Two volumes. Olten. 1966.

SIEGLER, HEINRICH VON. *Dokumentation zur Deutschlandfrage.* Two volumes. Bonn. 1961.

RECOMMENDED FURTHER READING

ALST, THEO VON. *Millionenspiele – Fernsehbetrieb in Deutschland.* Munich. 1972.

BAUSCH, HANS. *Organisation des Fernsehens und Rolle des Zuschauers.* Düsseldorf. 1972.

BURRICHTER, CLEMENS. *Fernsehen und Demokratie.* Bielefeld. 1972.

DEITERS, HANS-GÜNTER. *Fenster zur Welt, 50 Jahre Rundfunk in Norddeutschland.* Hamburg. 1973.

HAENSEL, CARL. *Rundfunkfreiheit und Fernsehmonopol.* Düsseldorf. 1969.

HÖFER, WERNER. *Fernsehen im Glashaus. Zur Kommunikation zwischen Programm und Publikum.* Düsseldorf. 1972.

JANK, KLAUS PETER. *Die Rundfunkanstalten der Länder und des Bundes.* Berlin. 1967.

MÜLLER-DOOHM, STEFAN. *Medienindustrie und Demokratie.* Frankfurt-am-Main. 1972.

Programmdirektion Deutsches Fernsehen/ARD. *Schlagwort: "Transparenz". Das Medium und sein Publikum.* Munich. No date.

PROKOP, DIETER. *Massenkommunikationsforschung* (2 vols.). Frankfurt-am-Main. 1971, 1973.

The contributions to the *Mainzer Tage der Fernseh-Kritik*, published annually by von Hase and Koehler Verlag, Mainz, under the general title: *Fernseh-Kritik.* The following have appeared to date:

1. STOLTE, DIETER. *Im Streit der Meinungen von Produzenten, Konsumenten, Rezensenten.* 1969.

2. STOLTE, DIETER. *Die gesellschaftskritische Funktion des Fernsehens.* 1970.

3. PRAGER, GERHARD. *Unterhaltung und Unterhaltendes im Fernsehen.* 1971.

4. FRANK, BERNWARD. *Fernsehen von morgen. Ende eines Monopolbewusstseins.* 1972.

5. HEYGSTER, ANNA-LUISE and SCHARDT, ALOIS. *Die verhinderte Wirklichkeit. Gewohnheit, Zwang, Tabu.* 1973.

(The sixth volume is at present in preparation.)

Name Index

Subject Index

Administrative council 10, 96f., 154, 162
chairmen of 16f.
BR 116
HR 102–103, 104
NDR 112, 121, 123–124, 130–133, 144, 146ff.
SWF 105–107
WDR 109, 110–111, 112, 121f., 129f.
ZDF 127f., 135
see also Supervision
Appointment of senior staff 134–137, 152
BR 115–116
HR 100, 103
NDR 112, 144, 146
SWF 105
WDR 110f., 128f.
ZDF 128f.
Apportionment (party-political) 79f., 82, 97, 121, 133, 134–137
NDR 144
WDR 129
ZDF 125, 127, 160
ARD 13–20, 22
chairmanship 19, 47
chairmen, *see* BAUSCH; HAMMER-SCHMIDT; SCHRÖDER
commissions/committees 20, 46–48, 55
constitution 18–20, 46
finance (budget, equalization) 21,

36f., 40, 45, 47, 50–51, 54–57, 91f., 170
founding 15f.
full assembly 19, 46, 171f.
guidelines, *see* DFS guidelines
membership 19, 23, 44
name 15–16
programme, *see* DFS
significance 21, 23f., 31ff., 38f., 42, 47–48, 85, 89, 91
technical institutions, 19, 44, 46
working assembly 19, 47, 88
yearbooks xii, 49
see also Commercial aspects; Taxation
ARD/ZDF 43–46, 53–54, 55, 57f., 61f., 65, 78f., 84, 93–94, 169

Basic Law 9, 14, 27ff., 143
Basic rights 3f., 9, 29, 137, 143
Bavarian Constitutional Court 114f.
Bavarian model of control 114, 118, 163f.
Bavarian plebiscite 3, 114–115, 118, 158ff.
Betriebsrat, *see* Personnel council
BR 14, 37, 40f., 45, 51, 55f., 58f., 62, 85, 135, 142, 154
intendant, *see* WALLENREITER
law 115–119
see also Administrative council; Appointment of senior staff; Broadcasting council; Intendant; Intendant elections

[193]